Takeover

Takeover

Race, Education, and American Democracy

DOMINGO MOREL

Oxford University Press is a department of the University of Oxford. It furthers
the University's objective of excellence in research, scholarship, and education
by publishing worldwide. Oxford is a registered trade mark of Oxford University
Press in the UK and certain other countries.

Published in the United States of America by Oxford University Press
198 Madison Avenue, New York, NY 10016, United States of America.

CIP data is on file at the Library of Congress
ISBN 978-0-19-067898-2 (pbk.)
ISBN 978-0-19-067897-5 (hbk.)

9 8 7 6 5 4 3 2 1

Paperback printed by Webcom, Inc., Canada
Hardback printed by Bridgeport National Bindery, Inc., United States of America

Para Mercedes, Kike, Lisa, Natalya y Camila.

Every generation does what it can.

—Antoinette Baskerville-Richardson

Newark

CONTENTS

CONTENTS

LIST OF FIGURES

LIST OF TABLES

I came to Newark in September 2012 as part of my dissertation research on the effects of state takeovers of local school districts on communities of color. In addition to doing research in Newark, I was also studying in Paterson and Union City, New Jersey. Like those in Newark, the Paterson schools were taken over by the state in the 1990s; Union City had been threatened but was able to avoid a takeover during the same period. Although my research was motivated by puzzles and questions concerning the political implications of state takeovers, over time, I became increasingly aware of the narrow focus of my research. The uneasiness that accompanied that awareness began when I attended a school board meeting in Newark that September.

At my first school board meeting in Newark, I sat in the back of the school auditorium. That evening, the first school board meeting of the 2012–2013 school year, there were roughly 150 people in attendance. Before coming to Newark, I had attended school board meetings in several cities, in several states. I had not seen this level of community participation in the previous meetings I had attended. However, I was struck when a speaker said that she was disappointed that given all of the issues in the school district, the auditorium was not filled to capacity. She mentioned that at the last meeting there had been standing room only and she had expected it to be the same that day. Although I was surprised to see so many people at a school board meeting, I was even more surprised to learn that there was an expressed disappointment in the low number of people that attended that meeting. The message was that *in Newark, we expect more.*

Indeed, after attending school board meetings for an entire year in Newark, I learned that there was more. On average, more than 200 people attended the monthly school board meetings in Newark that year. Moreover, the school board meetings were not just a place where school issues were discussed; they were community gatherings—even more, a community celebration. At that first meeting I attended, in addition to the school board, district officials, parents, and students in attendance, there was also a presence of community elders. The presence of community elders—former teachers, leaders of community organizations, volunteers—was a constant at every school board meeting. Elected officials and union leaders were also in attendance. Before that first meeting was called to order, as would be the case for every other meeting, the large crowd was boisterous and energetic. Clusters of people were spread throughout the room. I watched as the clusters of people hugged, talked, and laughed.

Every month, the board meetings were held at a different school throughout the city. Before the start of every board meeting, students from that respective school would perform for the audience. Some schools had band performances. Others had singers and dancers, while at others students performed poetry. The students proudly represented their schools to the broader community and brought cheers and laughter to the gathering before the community would then transition to official business. Once the meetings officially started, the festive atmosphere would give way to serious politics, where concern, anger, frustration, and disappointment would prevail for several hours before the meetings' conclusion. After each meeting, the clusters of people would come back together, debrief, argue, and laugh once again.

During my first meeting, as I sat in the back of the auditorium, I noticed a man diligently taking notes of the meeting. After the board meeting, I approached the man and introduced myself as a student doing research on the Newark schools, and the man responded by asking me, "Are you one of Cory Booker's peoples?" When I replied that I had never met Cory

Booker, Newark's mayor at the time, and clarified the focus of my research, he began to share that he, like many in Newark, was skeptical of outsiders and their "great plans to reform the schools in Newark." Although I was expecting to encounter resistance to an outsider's research agenda on the part of Newarkers—like I would and have experienced in every other city I have gone to study—I was mostly surprised by this man's view of Mayor Cory Booker. When I asked him several follow-up questions, including whether Mayor Booker came to the school board meetings, he said, "Booker only comes to staged events, and the school board meetings can't be staged, because these are real people here. So, Booker will not be around here." The man's critical remarks were representative of the opinions of others who attended the school board meetings, who shared their opinions publicly or in private conversations with me. Their opinion of their mayor contradicted the image of Booker that had been conveyed to the world outside of Newark.

Although I usually sat all the way in the back to try to observe as much as I could, during one meeting I sat down closer to the front. Next to me, there was a man with what appeared to be his two younger daughters. I quickly realized that the man was a person of prominence in Newark because many people were coming to say hello prior to the start of the board meeting. One individual embraced him and screamed to the crowd, "This is my mayor!" I then realized that it was Ras Baraka, son of the beloved Newarker Amiri Baraka, and the city councilman from the South Ward who would eventually run for mayor. In addition to serving as council member, Baraka was the principal of Central High School in Newark. When the board chair officially recognized Baraka, the audience roared. Together, the conversation concerning Booker and the Baraka encounter at the school board meetings further convinced me how *school politics is city politics*.

I had also noticed that for several meetings at the beginning of the school year, a woman by the name of Wafia Mohammed spoke during the public comments portion of the meeting and asked on behalf of Newark's Muslim community that the district recognize the Muslim Eid holidays, the same way other religious holidays are observed by the district. The board, which did not have the authority to decide on the school calendar, had conveyed to Ms. Mohammed that the decision was up to the state and the state-appointed superintendent.

Ms. Mohammed did not receive a response from the superintendent and for several meetings publicly made repeated requests for the observance. At the December school board meeting Ms. Mohammed once again approached the microphone and mentioned that the Muslim community had been asking politely for months to have the board adopt a policy that observes the holidays but had not heard anything in response. "So," she said, "we brought out our Muslim brothers and sisters tonight to let you know that we are here to fight. All of the Muslims in the room, could you please stand up?" Upon her request, seemingly the entire auditorium rose to its feet. Newark's Muslim community had come out in force to demand that their community be treated equally. That evening, most of the speakers on the list came to speak on the question of the Muslim holidays. However, even speakers who had signed up to talk about a myriad of other issues yielded their concerns to voice solidarity with the Muslim community in Newark.

At the April meeting, the community came out to defend their students. On April 9, roughly 500 students had walked out of school to protest Governor Christie's budget cuts, which were going to significantly affect the Newark schools. The students faced disciplinary actions from the district. During the meeting, the board introduced a resolution to support the students' right to civil disobedience. The resolution demanded that all of the students who faced school discipline and had anything placed on their school record as a result of the walkout should have their record expunged. The auditorium, which had roughly 400 people in attendance that evening, cheered in support of the board's resolution. One of the speakers that evening, Lawrence Hamm, received a strong ovation from the audience. Hamm, the chair of the People's Organization for Progress in Newark, had served on the Newark school board as a student in the early 1970s. As he approached the microphone, he yelled, "Power to the people," and, "No justice, no peace!" and the crowd joined in his call. Hamm, who had not attended a school board meeting in more than 30 years, said, "I came to support the student protestors and demand their amnesty.... We can't have our students learn about Martin Luther King Jr. and the civil rights movement and then punish them for doing exactly what Martin Luther King Jr. and the civil rights movement did!" The capacity crowd roared in approval.

Collectively, these observations, made over a year of studying Newark school politics, revealed a more poignant puzzle. As an outsider, I had come to study Newark's experience with the state takeover of its local schools, armed with data and narratives that the existing scholarship had provided. The dominant narrative was that Newark had failed to produce an adequate education for its children and state authorities had to intervene in a district that had failed to meet this basic requirement. The central claim in that narrative, explicitly and implicitly, was that the community and its local officials were not responsible and capable stewards of their children's education.

Indeed, the Newark schools have struggled. However, what I saw at the first school board meeting, and for every school board meeting after that, and every meeting I attended at a coffee shop, church, community agency, or home, revealed what seemed to be a counternarrative about the role of the community and its local officials in the Newark schools. These observations led to further questioning. In addition to understanding the political implications of state takeovers, the *reason* for state takeovers also merited examination. The dominant narrative that states take over school districts because of a community's inability to educate their children had not been critically challenged by the existing research. Perhaps the takeover occurred not because people didn't care—but precisely because they cared and demanded *more*. By caring, Newarkers may have set off a series of political struggles that had significant political consequences.

Can this thesis withstand the weight of social scientific inquiry? If so, is the Newark experience an outlier or representative of a broader experience shared by other communities of color, particularly black communities?

Or is Newark a harbinger for state-local relations in the United States? After all, Ken Gibson, Newark's first black mayor, once famously said, "Wherever American cities are going, Newark will get there first." These questions altered my research project, and the search for the answers to these questions became the focus of this book.

ACKNOWLEDGMENTS

This book began as a dissertation project at Brown University. As the book made its way through many stages and iterations, I have had the fortune of counting on the support and guidance of many people. It will be impossible to name everyone who has in some way contributed to this project, but I want to acknowledge some of the individuals who deserve special recognition.

I want to start by thanking my family. To my wife, Lisa, and daughters Natalya and Camila Morel, you are the coauthors of this project, and I cannot thank you enough for your boundless love and inspiration. To my parents Mercedes and Domingo and the rest of my family, Limary, Pedro, Alex, Charles, Lexi, Charlie, Cameron, Lilliam, Keyla, Mindy, Teolinda, Hector, Jafet, Keylis, Selene, Amelia, Luis, Midalma, Soyre, and Danny, thank you for all of your love and support.

I would also like to thank my friends who have been like family; their companionship has been important in this journey. Abraham, Matthew, Jason Dennis, Gene, Rob, Corey, Jason Delawrence, Tammy, Kenia, Rosie, Eddie, Joel, Julio, Ramon, Gerald, Frank, Sharon, Karoline, Joanna, Norelys, Shirley, Giza, Matt Lyddon, and Jennifer Nugent, I thank you.

I owe a great deal of gratitude to my academic family. First, I want to thank Marion Orr. You believed that I could transform from a community organizer to a scholar. Your endless support and guidance made that transformation possible. My family and I are eternally grateful for everything you have done for us. Susan Moffitt has also been a great mentor and friend. Every time I have needed advice about this book or about navigating our profession, you have always been there. I thank you for that. There have been others who helped shape this book in many different ways. Kenneth Wong was on my dissertation committee, and his advice and feedback were of great help. Additionally, at Brown, James Morone, Wendy Schiller, Corey Brettschneider, and Michael Tesler also provided constructive feedback, so I thank you. I am also greatly indebted to Mara Sidney, Patricia Strach, Sarah Reckhow, Jeffrey Henig, Stefanie Chambers, Peter Burns, Hahrie Han, Jamila Michener, Brandon Terry, Nyron Crawford, and Beth Schueler for your comments and your helpful conversations. Dr. Cynthia Hamilton has also been a great source of inspiration, so I thank you. I want to thank Angela Chnakpo at Oxford University Press for her guidance throughout the publication of this book. I would also like to thank the anonymous reviewers, whose comments helped improve this book.

Finally, thanks go to the people of Central Falls, Rhode Island, and Newark, Paterson, and Union City, New Jersey, for allowing me to learn about your experiences. Your persistence in the face of many challenges is a testament to the failures and promises of democracy in America.

Takeover

Schools, State, and Political Power

We will not accept Baltimore becoming a colony of the state, with its citizens having no say in the education of their children. African Americans, in particular, have fought a long, hard battle for equality. Over the years, too many paid the ultimate price for community empowerment.

—Community leaders following the state takeover of the Baltimore Public Schools, *Baltimore Sun*, April 1, 1997

In the United States, local governments have historically governed school districts. The responsibility of educating children has traditionally been placed on an amalgamation of local actors, including school boards, mayors, city councils, parents, and community groups. However, in the 1970s, state governments began to exert greater control over the local schools. By the 1980s, state takeovers of local school districts gained traction as a policy option for states. In 1989, New Jersey became the first state in the country to exercise the policy when it took·over the Jersey City Public Schools. Within 10 years, states took over another 39 school districts, including the Baltimore, Boston, Chicago, Detroit, and Newark public schools. By 2005, Cleveland, New Orleans, New York

City, Oakland, and Philadelphia would also experience a state takeover of their local schools.[1]

As of 2016, states have taken over more than 100 school districts, and hundreds more have been threatened to be taken over. States have cited concerns with poor academic performance to justify state takeovers of local school districts. Likewise, much of the scholarship on state takeovers of local school districts has focused on assessing the academic implications of state takeovers.

However, the focus on the educational implications of state takeovers is narrow and insufficient. The history of the development of education in the United States demonstrates that education is a political project, a result of political struggles between actors with competing interests and visions of education in America. Furthermore, as the quote from the Baltimore community leaders demonstrates, local communities have a stake in the governance of their schools.

This book examines the politics of state takeovers of local school districts. Although many major U.S. cities have experienced state takeovers, we know little about why states take over local schools and which communities are more likely to experience takeovers. We also lack a systematic understanding of how takeovers affect communities. Moreover, since takeovers introduce state actors into local governance, what effects do takeovers have on local governance? Since takeovers mostly occur in cities, what effect do state takeovers have on urban politics and our understanding of urban political theory? Finally, what do state takeovers teach us about democracy in America?

This book offers the first systematic study of state takeovers of local school districts. To assess the factors that contribute to state takeovers as well as the effects of takeovers on localities across the United States and over time, this study uses an original data set of nearly 1,000 school districts, including every school district that has been taken over by its respective state. The book also relies on case study analysis of several U.S. cities, with a primary focus on Newark, New Jersey. The state of New Jersey took over the Newark schools in 1995. As of 2017, the school district was still under state control. The mixed-method study consists of content analysis and more than 70 interviews with state commissioners of education, state legislators, mayors, city council members, school board members, teachers, parents, and community leaders.

STATE TAKEOVERS OF LOCAL SCHOOL DISTRICTS

State takeovers of local school districts emerged out of the accountability efforts in the 1980s (Wong and Shen 2003). Governors, who became increasingly involved with education, pushed state legislatures to pass laws that allowed state governments to take over underperforming school districts. As of 2017, at least 33 states in the United States have laws that allow state governments to take over their local school districts, and 22 states and the District of Columbia have taken over at least one school district.[2] In 2001, the federal government also authorized state takeovers of chronically underperforming school districts through the "corrective action" provisions of the No Child Left Behind Act (Manna 2011).

The expansion of state takeovers in the 1990s and early 2000s is also puzzling because the studies on the effects of state takeovers on academic achievement did not show that state takeovers of school districts markedly improved traditional educational outcomes such as reading and math test scores, school attendance, and graduation rates. At best, research on the effects of state takeovers on education outcomes during the period when takeovers grew as a policy option was mixed and inconclusive.[3] Despite the lack of evidence that state takeovers improved educational outcomes, states continued to rely on takeovers as an option. In 2015, state legislatures in Georgia and Wisconsin passed state takeover laws.[4] The state of Nevada, which passed a takeover law in 2003, also passed a new state takeover law in 2015.

Although scholars have examined the effects of state takeovers of local school districts on educational outcomes, we know less about the political implications of takeovers. In many cities, local communities and their leaders have seen the state takeover of the local school district as an assault by outside forces on their local autonomy (Green and Carl 2000; Oluwole and Green 2009; Orr 1999; Reid 2001). Following California's takeover of the Compton schools in 1993, community members called the state oversight a form of "slavery" (Reid 2001). In most cases, takeovers result in the abolishment of the locally elected school board, which has led some scholars to argue that takeovers violate the Voting Rights Act of 1965 (Green and Carl 2000).

In 2016, teachers and concerned citizens in Detroit organized several protests aimed at state authorities in Michigan. The state took over the Detroit Public Schools in 1999. In Detroit, state officials are responsible for school governance, including budget decisions. In May 2016, most of the Detroit Public Schools closed for two days when Detroit teachers called out sick in protest. Teachers organized the two-day "sick out" after they learned that many teachers were not going to be compensated because of the school system's budget woes.

The Baltimore, Compton, and Detroit examples illustrate that state takeovers of local school districts raise issues concerning federalism and state-local relations, allocation of resources, and governance authority. Since state takeovers introduce state actors into local governance decisions, questions of representation merit consideration as well. In other words, state takeovers are about political power. More specifically, this book will argue that state takeovers of local school districts are about race and political power.

In the pages that follow, the book will show that concern with underperforming schools was not the only motivation for state legislatures to pass laws to allow state governments to take over school districts. I will show that issues concerning resources, and *who* controlled those resources, were also significant factors that contributed to the emergence of state takeovers of local school districts. Thus, while the conversations concerning state takeovers of local school districts have focused predominantly on the failure of urban school systems to produce desired educational outcomes, this book is concerned with examining the political implications of state takeovers of local school districts. This is particularly important to the study of race politics in the United States because racialized communities have historically relied on education politics as a way to enter the public sphere. For marginalized communities, the path to political empowerment—and, as this book will argue, *disempowerment*—starts at the school level.

THE SCHOOLS AND POLITICAL EMPOWERMENT

Since the founding of the nation, leaders have recognized the role of the schools as providing students not only basic academic skills but also the knowledge and tools to maintain democratic institutions (Hochschild and Scovronick 2004). The public schools are part of the local institutions that Alexis de Tocqueville ([1835] 2007) argued "teach" Americans about community, citizenship, and the "spirit of liberty." For racial minorities, the schools have played a particularly important role in the process of political socialization and political empowerment.

Racialized communities relied on school-level politics to challenge state-sanctioned discrimination, which excluded people of color from participating in the political process (Katznelson and Weir 1985). The *Brown v. Board of Education* decision in 1954 not only provided the institutional delegitimization of Jim Crow but also helped provide momentum for the civil rights movement of the 1950s and 1960s. In the late 1960s and early 1970s, "community control" movements led by mostly African Americans and Latinos demanded that people of color have a greater voice in determining local policy, especially school policy (Kirst 1984; LaNoue and Smith 1973; Ravitch 2000).

By the 1970s, communities of color, particularly black communities, had gained political power in many U.S. cities. Although scholars and activists often point to the mayoral seat and seats on the city council as the standard for determining political power among African American and Latino communities, the reality is that the road to the mayoralty and the city council has often started with the ability to govern the schools. In their study of school reform in Atlanta, Baltimore, Detroit, and Washington, D.C., Henig et al. (2001) point out how school-related participation served as a catapult for the development of African American political power in these cities. Among Latinos, the school board has also been a key local institution for political empowerment. Latinos serve on school boards at higher rates than in any other political office (Hardy-Fanta et al. 2005; Shah 2006).

Thus, research has shown that the public schools are an important local political institution. The schools have provided the venue for citizens to engage in the public sphere when other venues of political participation have not been accessible. Moreover, in their pursuit of racial justice and political equality, racial minorities have looked at the local schools as the platform from which to launch their battle against systemic discrimination and subordination. In this respect, the schools have been the battering ram racial minorities have used to break through the barriers of political marginalization.

The school board has been of particular importance to black and Latino communities since it has served as the entry point for black and Latino political officeholders. As the research shows, the rise of black and Latino politicians in many cases begins at the school board. Therefore, an accurate assessment of a community's political empowerment must take into account how the school board fits into the overall constellation of political power. As states increasingly intervene in localities, and eventually take over local school districts, there are significant political implications for racialized communities in the local political ecosystem and beyond.

STATE TAKEOVERS AND AMERICAN POLITICS

In certain respects, state takeovers of local governments can be viewed from traditional perspectives in American politics. States have been in tension with cities since the emergence of cities. Throughout American history, we have seen how coalitions of nonurban state legislators have worked to curtail the power of central cities (Kantor 1988). Indeed, city politicians and state legislators representing urban constituencies have historically recognized the importance of minimizing state-local tensions and have worked to create alliances with political actors outside of their urban spheres to achieve political objectives (Bridges 1984; Burns et al. 2009). In his work on political machines, Steven Erie (1988) argues that powerful political machines emerged because of the intergovernmental alliances that local party leaders were able to forge with officials at the state and federal levels. Thus, the tension between state and local governments that eventually leads to a state takeover can be viewed from a perspective of contentious state and local relations in the United States.

Yet, while observers of American politics may be able to place state take-overs within a certain historical and political context, in certain aspects, state takeovers do not fit neatly into traditional conventions of American politics. In fact, state takeovers reveal puzzles concerning American race, state, and urban politics that surfaced following the tumult of the 1960s. The first puzzle the book explores concerns the effects of centralization and state takeovers on black and Latino representation.

Beginning in the 1960s, a number of factors began to emerge that allowed states to expand their powers. Federal grants sent to the states to address specific issues of education, poverty, and infrastructure, among other issues, helped states build capacity and expand their governmental reach in ways that were previously unfeasible (Hanson 1998; Hedge 1998; Manna 2006). Then in the 1970s and 1980s, the Nixon and Reagan administrations' "New Federalism" devolved decision-making powers to the states (Conlan 1998; Nice 1998; Reagan 1972). Under this new policy, programs that previously fell within the purview of the federal government were now under the authority of the states. As state governments became stronger, they expanded their role in local affairs and by the 1980s began to centralize authority over several policy areas, particularly public education (McDermott 2011).

By the late 1980s and early 1990s, several states began to take over local school districts. The takeovers shifted governance authority from local government to state government. As the state centralizes governance, what are the political implications for local communities? Despite the absence of a systematic study of state takeovers and their effects on local communities, the existing evidence suggests that takeovers are detrimental to local democracy. In cities such as Detroit, Baltimore, and Oakland, citizens have protested the takeovers, claiming that the takeovers dis-empower their communities (Ansell, Reckhow, and Kelly 2009; Epstein 2012; Orr 1999). Indeed, scholars of political participation have generally argued in favor of decentralized governance arrangements as a way to enhance democratic participation (Chambers 2006; Dye 1990; Fung 2004; Rivlin 1992).

Yet the focus on decentralization for the purposes of increasing polit-ical empowerment among racial minorities presents a puzzle. At times, the state has prevented racial minorities from achieving political power; and at other times, it has helped in the process of political empower-ment. Scholars have shown how federal and state disenfranchisement laws and mortgage and housing policies, among other things, contrib-uted to the political and economic marginalization of racialized com-munities (Pinderhughes 1987; Reed 1999). However, research also shows that racial minorities have relied on centralized authority to protect and advance racial equality and disrupt the policies and practices of local gov-ernment officials that have intentionally and unintentionally prevented racial minorities from achieving political power. As the political scien-tist Michael Dawson has pointed out, African Americans have generally supported a strong centralized state because of the "federal government's relative support in protecting black claims for property rights and human rights against public and private expropriators in the states and local com-munities" (2001, 26).

Although scholars have dedicated attention to understanding the role of government intervention in addressing barriers to political participation among historically marginalized populations, the scholarship has focused on federal intervention in states and localities. We know less about how state-level intervention at the local level affects racialized communities. Although it has been well documented that state governments have a poor record of advancing civil rights (Mettler 1998), we also know that on issues of race and civil rights, states and localities have unified in their opposi-tion to federal intervention (Lowndes 2008). As Dawson (2001) and other scholars have shown, marginalized populations have looked at state *and* local governments as equal culprits in their struggle for racial and social equality. Thus, the existing literature does not establish clear expectations for how the increasing presence of state governments in local affairs will affect communities of color.

Although contemporary studies of centralization and its effect on political empowerment suggest that decentralized arrangements are optimal for increasing empowerment, I argue that the "decentralization-as-optimal" argument ignores the complicated history that racial minorities have had with government. Instead, the book argues that the extent to which centralization is harmful or helpful is a function of how politically empowered a community is at the time of centralization. That is, state takeovers of local governments, as an act of centralization, will have different effects on communities that have higher levels of local political empowerment compared with groups with low levels of local political empowerment.

To assess the effects of centralized government on political empowerment among racial minorities, the book examines how state takeovers of local school districts have affected black and Latino descriptive representation on local school boards. The empirical investigation begins with a comparative case study of Newark, New Jersey, and Central Falls, Rhode Island. The state of New Jersey took over the Newark schools in 1995. Newark, like Detroit, and other cities that have experienced state takeovers of their local school districts share a similar political and economic history that has involved deindustrialization, racial tensions, and the eventual emergence of black-led urban regimes. By the time of the state takeover in Newark, the city had a black mayor and black majorities on the city council and school board.

In Central Falls, Rhode Island, Latinos represent the majority of the population. Unlike Newark, where African Americans had political power in the city at the time of the takeover, the city of Central Falls did not have any Latino political representation at the local level (mayor, city council, and school board) at the time the state took over the school district in 1991. As the case studies will show, the black community in Newark and the Latino community in Central Falls perceived and experienced the state takeover of their respective school districts differently. The case studies show that state takeovers can affect communities differently and reveal how state power works in and over marginalized communities.

To further test the empowerment argument, I provide a deeper historical analysis of Newark, to learn about the roots of the city's experience with the state takeover. In 1968, following civil unrest in Newark, the state considered taking over the Newark Public Schools to provide the city's black and Latino communities an opportunity to gain more political control of their schools. The politically marginalized black and Latino communities did not oppose a state plan to take over the school district, because they viewed the proposed intervention as a potential path to political empowerment. However, the state did not take over the local schools in 1968 but did in 1995, when blacks had political power and viewed the takeover as a threat to their political empowerment. Latinos, on the other hand, who had low levels of political empowerment at the time of the takeover, did not view the takeover as a threat. In fact, Latinos gained greater representation on the school board because of the takeover.

The results of the case study demonstrate that the dynamics of centralization are complex and help reveal potential causal mechanisms and hypotheses that I use to assess the effects of state takeovers beyond Newark. Following the Newark case study, the book employs quantitative methods to analyze the effects of state takeovers on black and Latino descriptive representation on school boards in every school district that experienced a state takeover between 1989 and 2013.

The empirical results suggest that state intervention has the capacity to address political marginalization at the local level by creating opportunities for previously excluded groups to participate in governance decisions. However, despite the potential to address political marginalization at the local level, the empirical results of this study also show that state takeovers can have detrimental effects on local communities and in ways previously not revealed. The results of the analysis show that takeovers have had the most negative effects on black communities, the group with the highest levels of political empowerment in cities that experienced state takeovers.

When states take over local school districts, state authorities adopt one of three possible options: (1) keep the elected school board, (2) abolish the locally elected board and appoint a new school board, or (3) abolish the locally elected school board and not replace it at all. The abolishment of locally elected school boards following a takeover has disproportionately affected black communities. By comparison, majority-white communities are less likely to experience a state takeover of their local school districts. Furthermore, in state takeovers of majority-white school districts, the takeover resulted in the abolishment of the locally elected school boards in only 4 percent of cases, compared with 33 percent in majority-black districts (see chapter 3 for details). In sum, black communities are more likely to experience the political disruption caused by the abolishment of locally elected school boards following a takeover.

As a result of these findings, the second question that emerges is, Why are black communities disproportionately negatively affected by state takeovers? Are academic concerns the driving factor for a state takeover of a local school district? Relying on historical and quantitative analysis, the book examines the factors that are associated with state takeovers of local school districts. To explain why state takeovers disproportionately affect black communities with higher levels of political empowerment, the book argues that two major factors emerged in the 1960s and 1970s that contributed to the rise of state takeovers: state centralization and black political empowerment in U.S. cities.

The emergence of state centralization in the 1960s and 1970s was facilitated by the rise of conservative, Republican-dominated politics at the state level. Republican governors passed most state takeover laws. The emergence of Republican-dominated state politics and its connection to the rise of state takeovers as a policy option is puzzling. The concept of local control has been a central idea in conservative and Republican politics. In other words, why would Republican state officials take the lead in proposing state takeover laws, and initiating state takeovers of local school districts, when ideological and conservative principles would suggest an approach that favors local control, rather than state centralization?

The book argues that political power and control of resources were the motivating factors behind the rise of state takeovers. As blacks gained political power in the 1960s and 1970s, demands for control of local

education policymaking and increased resources for local schools—
including lawsuits to increase funding for low-resourced communities—
began to change existing state-local dynamics. Republicans interested in
dismantling the civil rights gains of the 1960s found a path to political
power through state governments. Proponents of civil rights had focused
their attention on national and local government policies, which left an
opening for Republicans at the state level to exploit.

The rise of Republican-dominated state politics had significant political
consequences. In addition to shifting conservatives from a focus on decentralization to an embrace of centralization, black political empowerment
was met with resistance. As the foundation of black political empowerment, schools in the black community became a political target. Although
conservatives and small-government activists historically championed
local democracy and civic engagement, the participation among black
communities in the schools was politically problematic. As the theorist
Danielle Allen has noted, there is a distinction between "civic" and "political" engagement. Allen writes, "Civic is a safe word. It suggests public
action undertaken through approved venues and within the confines of
long-standing public agendas. 'Political' is a more charged term. It invokes
approved actions such as voting and holding office, but it also suggests
protest action, activism, and advocacy" (2016, 33).

For marginalized populations, particularly black communities, the
process of education has always been political. Decades of fights to provide
black students equal access to public schools and equal funding for low-
resourced public schools have required political struggles, not civic participation. In return, the response from the opposition was also political.
What emerged was a *conservative education logic*, promoted mostly, but
not exclusively, by Republicans and organizations such as the American
Legislative Exchange Council that professed to educate black children at
the same time that they invested in the political failure of the black community. As later chapters will show, it is within this political context that
state takeovers of local school districts emerged.

Following the historical examination, the empirical findings from
this study show that race, economics, and politics are equally important

factors associated with state takeovers. The findings show that increases in black political empowerment in cities are associated with the increased likelihood of a state takeover. The findings also demonstrate that increases in funding from federal and state governments for local school districts are also associated with the increased likelihood of a state takeover as well. The results of the study further show that black communities with high levels of political empowerment are more likely to experience the most punitive forms of state takeovers.

The final question the book examines is how the increasing presence of state governments in local affairs has altered urban politics and our understanding of urban political theory. It examines urban regime theory, the dominant urban political theory of the last 30 years. The book argues that although urban regime theory is still a relevant framework to analyze urban governance, the changing role of state actors, particularly governors, in urban regimes requires an expansion of urban regime theory as a conceptual framework. The chapter develops the concept of *cohesive* and *disjointed state-local regimes*. The concept proposes that local leaders can best represent the needs of their communities under cohesive state-local regimes, while localities are exposed to less desirable, even hostile, state-led policies under disjointed state-local regimes. The novel framework provides a tool to analyze state-local relations beyond state takeovers of local school districts. The framework can also be used to analyze the role of state governments in cities such as Flint, Michigan, for example, which endured a water crisis in 2016 because of negligent decisions on the part of state government.

The study of the political consequences of state takeovers reveals a narrative that is consistent with the scholarship in American politics that points to the democratic struggles of marginalized populations in the United States. This literature notes that periods of democratic gains among historically marginalized groups are also traditionally followed by responses that restrict democratic advancements. The growing scholarship on the American carceral state has been forceful in drawing a link between the democratic gains of the 1960s and the rise of mass incarceration in the 1970s to demonstrate support for this perspective (Alexander 2010; Burch 2013; Lerman and Weaver 2014; Weaver 2007; Western 2006).

In their work on the democratic implications of mass incarceration in the United States, Lerman and Weaver challenge the view that formal antidemocratic practices ended soon after the 1960s. Lerman and Weaver argue that the "criminal justice system has carved out an important exception to our democratic norms and, in so doing, has undercut the forward trajectory of equality and inclusion in America today" (2014, 6). The evidence and arguments presented in the coming chapters will suggest that the carceral state is not the only exception to American democratic norms. The systematic political disempowerment of black communities through the state takeover of local school districts shows how education has been central to the project of state-sanctioned political inequality.

PLAN OF THE BOOK

Chapter 2. A View from Two Cities

How do state takeovers affect communities? Chapter 2 looks at communities after state takeovers. The chapter provides an examination of how state takeovers have affected school policies and local politics in Newark, New Jersey, and Central Falls, Rhode Island. The chapter begins with an examination of the first five years following the takeover of the Newark schools (1995–2000) from the perspective of the city's black community, which had high levels of political power in the city at the time of the takeover. The chapter shows how the state takeover of the local schools had a devastating political and economic effect on the city's black community. Following the Newark study, the chapter focuses on a case study of Central Falls. The majority-Latino population in Central Falls experienced a state takeover of their local schools in 1991. Despite representing a significant portion of the city's population, the Latino community did not have any representation on the school board, on the city council, or in the mayor's office at the time of the takeover. The first Latinos to serve in public office in Central Falls were school board members appointed to the local school board by state officials after the takeover. Following appointments to the school board, Latinos won seats on the city council, and eventually, the city elected its first Latino mayor. The chapter argues that the state takeover of the Central Falls schools helped pave a path to local Latino political empowerment.

Chapter 3. State Takeovers and Black and Latino Political Empowerment

How is the representation of black and Latino communities affected by state takeovers of local government? Since racial minorities have had a complex history in the struggle between local autonomy and centralized authority, when does state centralization lead to increased political empowerment for racial minorities? Conversely, when does centralized authority negatively affect political empowerment among racial minorities? To answer these questions, chapter 3 focuses on state takeovers of local school districts. Specifically, the chapter examines how state takeovers of local school districts affect black and Latino descriptive representation on local school boards. Relying on a case study of Newark, New Jersey, and analysis of every state takeover of a local school district, the chapter shows that contrary to conventional wisdom, takeovers and centralization can increase descriptive representation among marginalized populations. On the other hand, the chapter also shows that under other conditions, takeovers are even more disempowering than scholarship has previously imagined and understood.

Chapter 4. Why Take Over?

Why do states take over local school districts? Additionally, why are Republicans—usually the champions of local control and decentralization—leading the efforts to take over local school districts? Finally, why do state takeovers disproportionally affect black communities? Relying on historical analysis, the chapter argues that several major factors in the 1960s and 1970s created the conditions that led to greater state centralization. The combination of greater state powers and the growth of black political empowerment in U.S. cities led to political tensions, which created an environment for state takeovers as an appealing policy option among state officials. Chapter 4 argues that political interests and control of resources were influential factors behind the rise of state takeovers. Republicans who were interested in dismantling the civil rights gains of the 1960s gained political power through state government, and takeovers were part of a political strategy to undermine black political empowerment. Following the historical analysis, the chapter examines the factors that increase the likelihood of a state takeover. Although concerns about academic performance are the main *public* justification for a state takeover, chapter 4 shows that increases in state and federal resources for local school districts, along with increases in black political empowerment, are associated with the decision to take over a district. The chapter makes the argument that race, politics, and economics are driving forces behind takeovers, not just low academic performance.

Chapter 5. The Implications of State Takeovers for Urban Politics

As states increase their presence in localities, what are the enduring implications for urban governance and theories of urban politics? Chapter 5 examines urban regime theory and argues that, though it is still a relevant framework, the changing role of state actors requires an expansion of urban regime theory as a conceptual framework. The chapter introduces the concept of cohesive and disjointed state-local regimes, which proposes that communities are better served and represented under *cohesive* state-local regimes.

Chapter 6. Takeovers and American Democracy

Chapter 6 discusses the implications of state takeovers. In cities that have experienced a state takeover of their local school district, educational outcomes have not improved in any significant way. However, state take-overs affect local politics in significant ways. In most cases, the takeovers have introduced dynamics that have altered local governance and the ways that local communities can influence policies that directly affect them. The chapter revisits the argument at the beginning of the book concerning the link between the schools and local political empowerment. Despite efforts to depoliticize education, education politics remain an essential compo-nent in the schema of local political empowerment. Finally, the chapter argues that takeovers reveal a flaw in the structure of American democ-racy that is only familiar to poor communities of color, particularly black communities. The book concludes by considering the implications of state takeovers beyond school systems.

A View from Two Cities

Newark, New Jersey, and Central Falls, Rhode Island

If the state had come in as a partner with us, I think [we] would
be talking about changes in urban education instead of a takeover.
—Eugene Campbell, former superintendent, Newark Public Schools,
quoted in Caryl Lucas, "Ousted Chief Quietly Exits the Stage,"
Star-Ledger, July 13, 1995

After the takeover, we came in, and there was a plantation mentality . . . . Those in power were the master in this plantation, and
they felt like the people were grateful to get what they got. Their
attitude was, "These people don't know what they don't know."
—School board member, Central Falls, Rhode Island

In the 1960s, as black communities throughout the United States fought
to dismantle barriers that denied blacks the right to full citizenship, the
city of Newark, New Jersey, was at the epicenter of the movement for
black political empowerment. In 1966, the Black Power activist Stokley
Carmichael visited Newark and told black Newarkers to take over the city,
"because it belongs to you" (Joseph 2015, 138). In 1967, Newark hosted the
first National Conference on Black Power. Between 1969 and 1970, black
community leaders, including Amiri Baraka, joined forces with Newark's

growing Latino community to create the Black and Puerto Rican Political Convention, which helped elect the city's first black mayor (Woodward 1999). In 1970, Newark became one of the first large U.S. cities to elect a black mayor. Thus, Newark occupies an important place in the history of black political struggle in the United States. However, we know little about how the story of the black community's struggle for political empowerment, its emergence as a political force in the city and in the state, and the efforts to disempower the community all converge in one place: the schools.

NEWARK, NEW JERSEY

Newark is the largest city in the state of New Jersey. As of 2010, it had a population of 277,140 (U.S. Census 2010). In addition to being the state's largest city, Newark has among the highest percentages of residents living in poverty in the state. Nearly 30 percent of Newarkers live below the poverty line. In 2010, the median household income in Newark was $34,387, compared with the state average of $71,637. Newark has also been disproportionately affected by high unemployment. Although the recession of 2008 was hard on the entire state of New Jersey, it was particularly hard on the city of Newark. In January 2010, the unemployment rate for the state of New Jersey was 9.72 percent, compared with 16.60 percent for the city of Newark (U.S. Bureau of Labor Statistics 2010).

African Americans and Latinos make up the majority of the city's population. African Americans represent 52 percent of the population, and Latinos represent 34 percent. Whites represent 12 percent of the population (see Table 2.1). Blacks have made up the majority of the population in Newark since the 1960s. Fueled by a migration from the South in the 1940s and 1950s, Newark's black population increased from 45,760 in 1940 to 207,458 in 1970 (Mumford 2007).

Upon their arrival in Newark, blacks encountered racial discrimination, which set a foundation for their status as unequal citizens for the decades

Table 2.1. NEWARK POPULATION BY RACE/ETHNICITY

Year	Total Population	Blacks (%)	Latinos (%)	Whites (%)
1970	382,417	54	12	34
1980	329,248	58	19	22
1990	275,221	58	26	16
2000	273,546	53	29	14
2010	277,140	52	34	12

SOURCE: U.S. Census.

that followed. As Tuttle notes, in Newark, "African Americans experienced what might be considered third-class citizenship, a rung below immigrants from eastern and southern Europe, who were themselves viewed as a separate caste from the older immigrant groups who basically ran the city" (2009, 149). As a group, blacks were the "last hired and first fired." Mobility around the city was minimal because blacks could not move to the suburbs (Cunningham 1966). Instead, discriminatory housing policies relegated blacks to the city's Central Ward (Mumford 2007). Discrimination in employment and housing also contributed to the community's political disenfranchisement.

By the mid-1960s, African Americans constituted the majority of the population in Newark. However, as of 1965, the city had only one African American elected official, and whites, whose percentage of Newark's population had decreased by nearly 50 percent between 1940 and 1970, remained in political control. In their efforts to gain political empowerment, blacks focused their attention on the local school board. Although blacks and Latinos had come to represent roughly 60 percent of Newark's population by the mid- to late 1960s, they represented 60 percent of the Newark student population as early as 1961 (Lilley et al. 1968). By the late 1960s, blacks and Latinos represented 74 percent of the students in the Newark public schools (Rich 1996). Yet representation on the school board did not reflect the community's racial and ethnic makeup. At the beginning of 1967, there was only one African American and no Latinos on the school board.

In the summer of 1967, racial tensions escalated in Newark when a school board seat became vacant and the city's black community expected Mayor Addonizio to appoint an African American to fill the vacancy. The black community, led by the local branch of the NAACP, had pushed Addonizio to appoint Wilbur Parker, an African American and the city's budget director, to fill the vacancy (Rich 1996). However, Addonizio appointed James Callaghan, a white Newark council member, to fill the position (Tuttle 2009). Following the news of Callaghan's appointment, Fred Means, the president of the Negro Educators of Newark, said, "The Negro community is in turmoil over this injustice. If immediate steps are not taken, Newark might become another Watts" (Lilley et al. 1968, 15). One month later, at Callaghan's nomination hearing, one speaker "predicted that 'blood would run through the streets of Newark,' if Callaghan was named to the post at tonight's meeting" (Mumford 2007, 104).

The Board of Education decided not to confirm Callaghan's nomination, and that decision prevented further escalation. However, roughly two weeks later, the community's frustration with their persistent subordinate status did lead to unrest in Newark. On July 12, 1967, the city of Newark erupted in one of the deadliest urban uprisings in the history of the United States. The beating of a black taxicab driver by white Newark police officers pitted the city's black community against the white power structure. Although it is commonly described as the "1967 Newark Riot," many Newarkers, particularly black Newarkers, refer to the incident as a "rebellion." For six days in mid-July, Newark's black community clashed with Newark police, state troopers, and the National Guard. In the end, 26 people were killed, 23 of whom were African American (Herman 2005).

In the wake of the 1967 unrest, the governor of New Jersey commissioned a report on "civil disorder" in the state. The report attributed the controversial Callaghan nomination as one of the factors that "helped set the stage for the July riot" (Lilley et al. 1968, 15). In addition to referencing lack of representation on the school board as a key factor, the report also cited the "state of educational crisis" in the Newark public schools. In 1967, Newark third graders were reading at two grade levels below the "national norm." The dropout rate was at 32 percent (Lilley et al. 1968, 77).

The report also cited dilapidated buildings and a shortage of teaching personnel as factors contributing to the education "crisis" in Newark. Equally as troubling, the report showed that by the mid-1960s the Newark public schools did not have the physical space to educate every Newark student.

The lack of representation on the school board, their inability to have a voice in school policies, and the severe shortage of the resources required to educate black children in Newark led the black community to mount a political response to what they perceived was a political obstruction to their participation and their children's education. In addition to fighting to gain a greater voice in the education of their children, local leaders also recognized the importance of securing additional resources for the schools. Local political officials, community leaders, and their allies in Newark and other cities in New Jersey mobilized to address the lack of resources and educational opportunities that was contributing to poor educational outcomes in the urban and predominantly black schools. The demands for a greater voice and resources set the black community in Newark on a path to collide with an entrenched political opposition in the state of New Jersey.

By the early 1970s, the transition to a black-led local political regime had begun in Newark. In the 1970 municipal election, Newark elected three black city council members as well as the city's first black mayor, Kenneth Gibson (Rich 1996). In addition, during the 1970–1971 school year, nonwhites represented the majority on the school board for the first time in the city's history (Tuttle 2009). As blacks gained political power in Newark, their influence grew in New Jersey's state politics. As Newark was the state's largest city, in one of the most vote-rich counties in New Jersey, Newark's black political leadership gained influence beyond city limits, which local leaders utilized to bring resources to the city.

In addition to gaining political control of local institutions, black citizens in the largest urban communities in New Jersey challenged schooling disparities in the courts. In 1970, plaintiffs filed a suit on behalf of Kenneth Robinson, a student in Jersey City's public schools, which argued that New Jersey's system of funding public schools was unconstitutional. The plaintiffs argued that the system's heavy reliance on local property taxes created a disadvantage for students from poorer communities (Tractenberg 1974). In 1973, the state's Supreme Court ruled in *Robinson v. Cahill* that the state's funding system was unconstitutional because it failed to provide students from poorer districts a "thorough and efficient" education as mandated by the state's constitution. Despite the court's decision to change the funding formula, state legislators refused to act on the order. However, urban legislators eventually led the push to approve a new funding formula that increased state funding for urban school districts (Salmore and Salmore 2013). Between 1975 and 1977, the state's contribution to support public education increased by nearly $450 million (Yaffe 2007).

Despite the increases in funding, in 1981, the Education Law Center, based out of Newark, filed a lawsuit claiming that *Robinson v. Cahill* did not fundamentally address the funding gap between urban and suburban schools. In 1985, the state Supreme Court issued the first ruling in the *Abbott v. Burke* case, deciding in favor of the plaintiffs, and ordered the Office of Administrative Law to remedy the state's unequal funding of school districts. The decision and the subsequent *Abbott* cases had significant educational, economic, and political implications. The New Jersey legal community considered the decision "the most important state court decision of the Twentieth Century," and the *New York Times* described it as "the most significant education case" since the 1954 *Brown v. Board* decision (Tractenberg, Liss, and Sadovnik 2005).

In Newark, local leaders viewed the court victories as a positive outcome in a decades-long struggle to improve the schools. Although educational outcomes had improved since the late 1960s, the district still had significant challenges. In the early 1990s, the district's graduation rate was only at 54 percent, and only roughly 25 percent of all 11th-grade students had passed every section of the state's high school proficiency tests (McLarin 1994). However, education advocates and Newark school administrators viewed the increase in resources for the city schools as the first significant effort in the state and city's history to address racial educational inequities in Newark.

The new funding formula provided increased funding for Newark and other urban districts in the state. At a June 1990 Newark school board meeting, Superintendent Eugene Campbell reported to the board that because of the *Abbott* court decision that same month, "28 districts would be receiving a significant increase in funds. The children of New Jersey stand to benefit by this change in funding to school districts in need."[1]

At the same time, opposition to the increased funding grew within the state's wealthier districts, whose residents resented increased taxes on the state's wealthier communities. John Dorsey, the Republican senate minority leader from Morris, one of the wealthier districts in New Jersey, stated that the new funding formula required "working class people in middle class communities who drive around in Fords to buy Mercedes for people in the poorest cities because they don't have cars" (Salmore and Salmore 2013, 321). The resentment was also noticeable along racial lines, since the demands for increased funding were led by black political leaders on behalf of mostly black and Latino students in cities such as Newark.

In response, legislators from the wealthier districts demanded the implementation of accountability measures. Therefore, the "thorough and efficient" law provided increased funding for school districts, but it also created a monitoring regime as well. Legislators incorporated mechanisms that would monitor not only student academic achievement but also district governance and fiscal management. It was the first time in the state's history that student academic achievement and district governance would come under such scrutiny.

The intensified attention that came with the additional resources presented political and economic challenges for Newark. In Newark, the school district had been part of a system of patronage for decades. Since the 1930s, the public school system had become a major employer for the city of Newark (Anyon 1997). Fueled by the Great Depression and the rapid decline of industry, the schools became a stable source of employment for the city's residents. The school district provided jobs for the city's dominant Irish and then Italian populations. When African Americans represented the majority of the city's population and the majority in the local political regime, political and school officials hired black Newarkers, and by the 1980s, blacks represented the majority of district employees.

Just like the ethnic groups before them, blacks depended greatly on the school system for jobs.

In some instances, local officials engaged in corrupt practices that led to their imprisonment. In 1988, Malcolm George, a Newark school board member, was indicted for extorting money from two Newark teachers in exchange for job promotions. Samuel A. Alito Jr., the U.S. attorney for New Jersey at the time, charged George with using his position and "considerable influence" to extort the teachers (Rangel 1988).

The corruption charges were used by political opponents to bolster their arguments about Newark officials being careless, irresponsible, and incapable of administering the school district. Charges of patronage were also levied against the district. As a result, hiring community members to work in the district, a practice that had developed as an essential part of the city's economic development for decades, came under political attack. Marion Bolden, a native Newarker who taught in the district for more than two decades and eventually served as district superintendent, said that the charges of patronage were detrimental to the community and unfair. She added that

> as a superintendent, you can be hard and fast about principalships. I believe this. You can say to the board, "No, that is the one position where I need to have the best person." There is no negotiating there. But who cares if you get a parent liaison that is recommended by the board? I understand that parents need jobs, and so if they are going to do the job, give them the job. My thing was, I want a community person hired first. It makes sense. I want people from the community in the schools because it is their children. What's wrong with the security guard being from Newark? And the parent liaison and the cafeteria staff being from Newark? Why are you giving these jobs to somebody else? That is not patronage; that is community.[2]

By the 1980s, state officials in New Jersey had increased their monitoring of the Newark school district, and by the late 1980s, they had the political and policy tools to intervene in unprecedented ways. In 1988, the state of New Jersey became the first state in the country to pass a "takeover" law, which allowed the state's Department of Education to take over a school district for failure to demonstrate improvement. By the late 1980s, the Newark school district faced the threat of a takeover. As chapter 5 will demonstrate, Newark's influence in statewide politics helped prevent a takeover in the late 1980s. However, following the election of Christine Todd Whitman, a Republican, as governor in 1993, the threat of a takeover of the Newark schools gained momentum.

Once elected, Whitman declared that "improv[ing] the financial accountability of public schools" would be a top priority for her administration, since school budgets had become the "costliest government venture" in New Jersey (Mondics 1993). Whitman charged her commissioner of education, Leo Klagholz, with controlling public school spending in the state. As the state's largest school district, which received roughly 75 percent of its funding from the state, Newark gained the most attention from the Department of Education. Soon after his confirmation as commissioner, Klagholz expanded the state's monitoring of the Newark school district.

Klagholz ordered a "comprehensive compliance investigation" of the Newark school district—a process mandated by the state when a district is deemed unable to resolve its deficiencies internally. The comprehensive compliance investigation focused on three key areas: educational programs, fiscal practices, and governance and management (McLarin 1994). The resulting 1,798-page report cited nearly 100 complaints including the lack of resources in the schools, school buildings in disrepair, cafeteria workers not providing adequate "portions" of food to students, teacher shortages, and administration and school board mismanagement of the district. The authors of the report stated that the "Newark School District has been at best flagrantly delinquent and at worst deceptive in discharging its obligations to the children enrolled in the public schools" (State of New Jersey Department of Education 1994, 9).

Following the release of the report, Commissioner Klagholz made the formal recommendation to the state Board of Education that the state takeover the Newark schools. In their argument to the state board, Klagholz and leaders at the Department of Education stated that, "given the pattern of the last 10 years, it is unlikely that the district's same leadership, however well-intentioned, can demonstrate the ability . . . to produce major change" (Turcol and John-Hall 1994).

The Newark school board appealed the decision. However, the state Board of Education voted 9–1 to move forward with the takeover. Interestingly, the state board used the same rationale to take over the school district that Newark leaders had used to demand greater resources from the state. In its decision to take over the Newark schools, the board stated, "Given the record here and the right of the students of Newark to a constitutionally adequate education, the tired excuses and promises to do better in the future which the Newark board is now offering us are not sufficient" (Reilly 1995).

Newark political leaders challenged the state's justification and reasoning for the takeover. Mayor Sharpe James said that he did not "believe that a unilateral takeover of the board of education is the answer, especially since there is no evidence of any significant academic improvement among students in Paterson and Jersey City, where the state is already running the school districts" (Nix 2015). Charles Bell, a Newark school board member at the time of the takeover, accused the state of not abiding by its own takeover law, which allowed districts to have a hearing to challenge the merits of the takeover. Bell said that the state's refusal to follow procedure was a "continuation of the whole process of the state being the judge, jury and prosecutor" (B. Carter 1995). Indeed, the only member of the state Board of Education to vote against the takeover, S. David Brandt, based his decision on those same grounds. Brandt, the only attorney on the state board at the time, voted against the takeover because he agreed with Newark's contention that the district deserved a full hearing in court (Reilly 1995). Despite the appeal by Newark leaders, on July 12—ironically, the same day the Newark rebellion started 28 years earlier—the state officially took over the Newark school district. The schools, which provided the platform for blacks to mobilize for empowerment in Newark, also

provided the platform from which the biggest threat to black empowerment would be launched.

In the weeks leading up to and immediately following the takeover,
the state took great care in avoiding the appearance of a "hostile" takeover of the Newark schools. Klagholz stated that the takeover "will not
mean the disenfranchisement of the people in Newark" (Reilly 1995).
State officials worked with the soon-to-be-fired Superintendent Eugene
Campbell to ensure that the transition of authority would not provide
any optics that would confirm the perception of many Newarkers: of
white state officials aggressively removing black school leaders from
their jobs. Indeed, state officials were successful in avoiding the appearance of a hostile takeover. Superintendent Campbell and 12 other top
district officials vacated the central office with little fanfare on July 12,
1995 (Lucas 1995).

Following the takeover, the state's appointment of an African American
superintendent was also part of the effort to avoid seeming like a "colonization" of a majority-black school district. Beverly Hall, who was
appointed the superintendent of Newark schools after serving as deputy
chancellor of the New York City Public Schools, was well aware of black
resentment toward the takeover. In a response to the criticism that she was
a "tool of a white state leadership," Hall said, "When they get to know me,
they will not use the phrase 'plantation mentality'" anymore (Larini 1995).
Thus, the appointment of an African American superintendent and efforts
to ensure a "smooth" transition of authority were coordinated steps on the
part of the state officials to avoid seeming as if they were performing a
hostile takeover of the Newark school district.

However, behind the scenes, the takeover did seem hostile to some.
School administrators complained about not being properly notified of
their termination. One of the fired employees said that the way the state
handled the terminations showed "no respect." He added, "This is no way
to treat an employee. I'm not mad about being fired. Tell me my rights"
(Peterson 1995). Another school official added, "The takeover was not
pleasant, but takeovers as takeovers are, are not a pleasant thing. The state

sent in two officials who were responsible for the dirty work of terminating people, and they were just so mean-spirited. It was a hostile takeover."[3]

In addition to removing the superintendent and other top school officials, state officials abolished the locally elected school board and replaced it with an advisory board. Again, the state officials attempted to avoid a perception of colonization, which in their view would have undermined their claims of legitimacy. As a result, Klagholz, who was responsible for appointing members to the advisory board, sought to assemble an advisory board that was "representative of the grassroots community" (Larini, Reilly, and Peterson 1995). After reviewing hundreds of applications, the commissioner decided on a 15-member board that descriptively represented the city: 53 percent African American (eight members), 27 percent Latino (four members), and 20 percent white (three members) (Walker 1995).

As will be discussed in chapter 3, the abolishment of the elected board had differing effects on the African American and Latino communities. For blacks, who controlled the majority of the school board before the takeover, the switch from an elected to an appointed board signified a decrease in symbolic *and* substantive power. The notion of an "advisory board" had a negative effect on African Americans because prior to the takeover they controlled the school board and had significant influence on issues related to district governance, budget, and personnel.

At the same time, the fact that African Americans maintained a majority on the advisory board and that the state appointed a black superintendent seemed to neutralize the issue for some in the black community, particularly the teachers union and other district employees. By the 1990s, African Americans represented the majority of teachers and district staff in the Newark schools and were an integral component of the black political base in the city. However, many teachers did not feel threatened by the takeover and believed that the state was going to partner with the teachers union to improve education in Newark. These acts essentially "bought" the state time. According to one high-level school administrator at the time of the takeover:

People didn't know what was going to happen. A teacher in a distressed school was happy about the takeover. In a high-achieving school, many were thinking, "They are not going to hurt us." And when Beverly Hall came in, one of the first things she did was clean the graffiti in every building. She got rid of it. So it wasn't all bad. But it began to get negative when the principals were evaluated and their leadership was questioned. That's when it started to get bad. That's when people began to feel like someone came into their home and they weren't being respected.[4]

Although some in the black community supported the superintendent and argued that she deserved an opportunity to prove herself to the community, by 1996, things started to change. The Republican-controlled state legislature proposed to cut nearly $32 million from the district's budget (Kukla 1996). Newark's superintendent and state officials proposed a plan that led to drastic layoffs in Newark. The state's efforts to decrease the school-related workforce in the city had the most severe consequences for the city's black community.

Although some in Newark believed that the state takeover was going to lead to greater state support for the district to improve education, it became increasingly clear to many that the takeover was not just about educating the children in Newark. School funding, and who controlled those resources, was also a major factor in the decision to take over the district.

Although federal and state aid to cities began to decline in the 1980s, school funding was one of the few areas where cities received increased funding. The school system, which had been a source of economic development for the city of Newark, and one of the few areas in city politics where outside resources (state and federal) had actually increased in the 1980s and 1990s, was removed from the control of the local community and its political leaders by the mid-1990s. As one Newark community leader said about the takeover:

When Ken Gibson was the mayor, he didn't have 100 percent support of the business community, and he didn't have support of the political "in"-group. He was an outsider. So he created a base . . . , and one of the few areas that he could actually penetrate in terms of patronage was the school district. So the district became sort of a patronage. Sharp James probably perfected that, and the local school board became a political arm of Newark politics. So there's no doubt there that the state takeover was to try to undo that.[5]

Immediately following the takeover of the Newark school district, the state fired 13 high-level school officials, including the superintendent, Eugene Campbell. Among the 13 officials, there was one white and one Latino, and the remaining 11 were African Americans. In the summer of 1996, another round of layoffs, this time more severe, would take place in the school district. Again, blacks were the most negatively affected by the layoffs. Following her termination, one African American district employee said, "I don't believe [the state takeover] is geared to help the children. The state is laying off more Blacks and replacing us with white males" (Lucas 1996).

When rumors started to circulate in 1996 that the state was going to drastically cut the district budget, which would result in cuts to programs and district staff, the community turned out in force. At the May 1996 advisory school board meeting, the community turned out in large numbers to protest the proposed budget cuts. That night, 45 people spoke at the meeting. It was by far the highest turnout since the state had taken over the district. The majority of the speakers, who included civic leaders and elected officials, focused their remarks on concerns with cuts to school programs as well as the privatization of school services in the district.[6]

On July 19, 1996, the rumors many had feared were confirmed when Superintendent Beverly Hall and state officials fired more than 600 district employees. According to Hall, the district had to shift focus from being a local employer to being a student-centered institution. In an editorial published by the *Star-Ledger*, Hall stated:

Because the Newark district has been primarily a source of jobs rather than an educational institution, the reorganization requires a shift of resources from unnecessary noninstructional jobs to instructional and student services. To fund $26.3 million in upgrades for students and eliminate gross inefficiencies will require an overall reduction of 674 positions (some vacant), resulting in a total of 634 layoffs, or 7% of the district workforce. Of those, 124 positions will come from the central office, 406 positions will be eliminated through efficiency measures, 122 nonteaching positions will be eliminated through changes in each building and 22 nonbudget positions will be discontinued. The reorganization plan reflects hard decisions needed to put children first. (Hall 1996)

The job cuts were devastating to many Newarkers who relied on the school district for employment. Also, contrary to the depiction portrayed by state authorities to justify the takeover, of rampant corruption and patronage on the part of Newark politicians securing high-salary positions for their friends, the overwhelming number of cuts were to low-salary employees. Among the laid-off employees, 160 were school bus attendants; 117, cafeteria workers; 72, teacher aides; and 50, clerks (Chiles 1996). The Newark Teachers Union president, Joseph Del Grosso, referred to the mass termination of employees as the "Beverly Hall Massacre" (Chiles 1996).

An examination of the Newark school district's professional employment data shows that African Americans were the most negatively affected by these layoffs. Between 1996 and 1998, there were small differences in the number of administrators (central office employees, principals, and assistant principals) who were terminated (see Figure 2.1). There was an actual increase in the number of black administrators from 1996 to 1998. There was also a small increase in the number of white administrators. On the other hand, there was a decrease in Latino administrators from 31 in 1996 to 24 in 1998.

However, there were differences among the groups in the termination of teachers and professional support staff. Between 1996 and 1998, 137 fewer black elementary and secondary teachers were employed by the district, representing a 5 percent decrease among black teachers from 54 percent to 49 percent (see Figure 2.2). By comparison, between 1996 and 1998, the white teacher population increased by 2 percent. The Latino elementary and secondary teacher population also increased by 2 percent, from 108 to

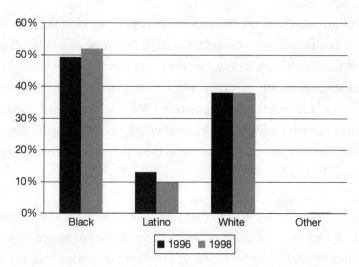

Figure 2.1. Newark District Administrators by Race/Ethnicity, 1996–1998
SOURCE: N.J. Department of Education and Newark Schools, "Certificated Staff."

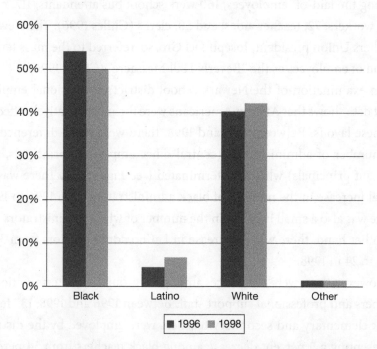

Figure 2.2. Newark Elementary and Secondary Teachers by Race/Ethnicity, 1996–1998
SOURCE: N.J. Department of Education and Newark Schools, "Certificated Staff."

158 between 1996 and 1998. African Americans also constituted the majority of cuts to the professional support staff. Between 1996 and 1998 there was a decrease of 102 black support staff, compared with a decrease of 56 for whites. There was a slight increase of Latino support staff (13) throughout this period.

In addition to the cuts in professional jobs, there were cuts to other full-time employees. Between 1996 and 1998, the state administration cut 447 full-time jobs in the Newark Public Schools. Blacks represented 60.4 percent of these cuts, compared with 30.2 percent for whites and 11.6 percent for Latinos. Despite the significant cuts to the full-time jobs, the biggest cuts came to the employees who worked part-time for the district. Here again, blacks represented the majority of these cuts. From 1996 to 1998, the state eliminated nearly 2,000 part-time jobs in the Newark Public Schools. African Americans represented 57.2 percent of these cuts, compared with 32.6 percent for whites and 10.2 percent for Latinos.

In sum, the state takeover of the Newark schools had a significant effect on the community, which depended on the jobs the district provided. As the largest group in Newark, with the deepest connections to the public schools, the African American community was the group most negatively affected by the job cuts. Although state officials justified the cuts by arguing that they would lead to "improved instruction" in Newark, many argued that the cuts undermined important gains the school district was making by cutting programs that helped support students. For instance, the state reduced the number of social workers in the Newark schools. The social workers provided multiple services to the students, including supporting teachers in the classroom and "counseling children with personal problems ranging from shyness and loneliness to sexual abuse and homelessness" (Goodnough 1996). The cuts also affected programs that provided mentoring to students to reduce violence and suspensions, prevent student dropout, and decrease teen pregnancy.[7] Indeed, in the five years following the takeover, student suspensions increased by 30 percent (see Figure 2.3). Moreover, in a number of key areas, including high school proficiency test scores and

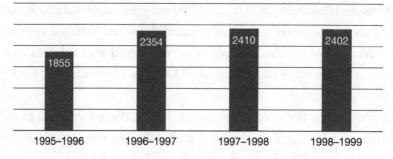

Figure 2.3. Student Suspensions in Newark Public Schools, 1995–1999
SOURCE: Association for Children of New Jersey, "Newark Kids Count 2000: A Profile of
Child Well-Being," http://acnj.org/downloads/2000_01_01_NewarkCityReport.pdf.

graduation rates, student academic performance worsened in the five
years following the takeover (Association for Children of New Jersey
2000). In addition to terminating workers and cutting programs, the
state takeover also led to the abolishment of the locally elected school
board. The next chapter provides an analysis of the effects of the takeover on school board representation in the city.

The first five years of the takeover were turbulent for Newark. The
hostile removal of district officials, the abolishment of the elected
board, and the firing of more than 600 full-time staff members and
more than 2,000 part-time staff members created a strained relationship between the city's majority–African American population and the
state administration. The takeover was a major setback for a community that had fought for greater political empowerment, particularly to
address concerns with the education system. In 1967, black Newarkers
rebelled against an oppressive local political structure and a school system that was failing to educate their children. By the mid-1970s, black
Newarkers finally represented majorities in city government. By the
1980s, the city along with other urban centers in the state were finally
promised the resources to improve the schools. Yet at the same time—
the mid-1980s—the state informed the city that they were not meeting education standards and threatened the district with a takeover.
In 1995 the state took over the Newark schools because local leaders
"were not capable" of delivering an adequate education to the children

of Newark. Following the takeover, Eugene Campbell, the outgoing superintendent, said:

> I don't feel good—having started in the district as a teacher and being born in Newark and graduating from the school system . . . . [A]s an educator, father, and grandfather, there are changes in Newark and other school districts that need to be made for African-Americans, Hispanics, and poor whites . . . . In the school system, there are pockets of success. You find schools in our district that work very well, but you find schools in our district with students in great need . . . . I think if the state had come in as a partner with us, I think [we] would be talking about changes in urban education instead of a takeover. (Lucas 1995)

CENTRAL FALLS, RHODE ISLAND

> Last year we were afraid to speak up. We were confused about the issues. This year we have been present in the school almost every day. We have attended meetings. We have seen firsthand what goes on in the high school . . . . We have grown in knowledge and in courage.
> —Central Falls parents' statement to the Rhode Island
> Board of Regents, January 6, 2011; my translation

At the January 2011 meeting of the Rhode Island Board of Regents—the governing body of the Rhode Island public schools—a group from the city of Central Falls stood up and read a prepared statement in Spanish during the public comments portion of the meeting. The group, consisting mostly of parents, attended the meeting to demand improvements from the education system. A year before, the Central Falls School District received national attention after the school board and superintendent decided to fire the entire teaching and administrative staff at the "chronically low-performing" high school (Greenhouse and Dillon 2010). The firings were spurred by a disagreement between the teachers union and the district

administration on a School Improvement Grant intervention plan targeted at the low-performing school.[8]

Following the spectacle of the teacher firings in Central Falls, an
intense debate ensued, locally and nationally, about the merits and failures of school reform and the intervention methods designed to improve
low-performing schools. Less attention, if any at all, was dedicated to
understanding how state and federal interventions in the Central Falls
schools affected parents and other members of the community. As the
quote above demonstrates, parents and members of the Central Falls community responded to the ordeal that followed the intervention by becoming increasingly involved at the school and in the process had "grown in
knowledge and in courage."

The Central Falls parents' participation in the Board of Regents meeting
is revealing in a number of ways. First, it demonstrates how the schools
can provide the venue for political socialization. As the quote points out,
these particular parents went from being "afraid to speak up" to becoming
fully engaged in the school. Central Falls is a city with a majority-Latino
population. Most of its residents are first-generation immigrants primarily from Colombia, Guatemala, and the Dominican Republic.[9] Thus, for
these parents and others in the community, the schools have provided a
forum for political engagement.

Second, the Board of Regents meeting did not take place in Central
Falls. The meeting was in Narragansett, Rhode Island, nearly an hour
south of Central Falls. The fact that parents would travel this distance for
a school-related meeting is somewhat surprising given the typical complaints of community apathy regarding school matters. Not only were the
parents present; they were organized. The parents organized carpools, collectively worked on the prepared statement, prepared copies for the Board
of Regents and the audience at large, and designated one of their own as
spokesperson.

The parental and community mobilization had been a result of an ongoing process, years in the making in the Central Falls School District. Over
the past two decades, Central Falls had undergone a steady transition that
involved an increase in the number of Latino school board members and

an increase in the number of Latino school administrators. Over time, the school board and the administrators had been developing a stronger link between the schools and the community, and the parental presence at the Board of Regents meeting in Narragansett was a manifestation of that ongoing process (Morel and Cassidy 2011). Perhaps most surprising is that all of this occurred while the school district was under state control. The state of Rhode Island had taken over the Central Falls School District in 1991 (Espinosa 1991).

Central Falls is the smallest city in the state of Rhode Island. However, with a population of nearly 20,000, it ranks as one of the most densely populated cities in the United States.[10] The city is located five miles north of Providence and is part of the greater Providence metro area. In the 19th century, Central Falls became a manufacturing center. Irish, French Canadian, and Scottish immigrants arrived in Central Falls to work in the textile mills. By the early to mid-1900s, Poles, Portuguese, Cape Verdeans, and Azoreans had migrated to the city as well.

However, by the 1970s the manufacturing industry began to disappear in Central Falls, which led to demographic shifts in the city. New immigrant groups, mainly from Latin America, replaced the older immigrant groups that left the city. In the 1970s and 1980s, Colombian immigrants began to settle in Central Falls. By the 1990s, migrants from other Latin American areas, including Puerto Rico, the Dominican Republic, and Guatemala, settled in Central Falls as well. The number of immigrants from Latin America to arrive in Central Falls and the greater Providence area grew by more than 300 percent between the 1980s and the 1990s, making it one of the largest immigrant destinations in the United States (Pew Hispanic Center 2002). By 2000, Latinos represented nearly half of the city's population.

Although the Latino population in Central Falls had grown significantly since the 1970s, as of 1990, Latinos did not have any political representation in the mayor's office, on the city council, or on the school board. Whites, who had dominated the city's politics, maintained political control of the city even as their population declined and the Latino population increased. Following a similar trajectory as other racialized communities in the United States, the path to political empowerment for the city's Latino community went through the schools. However, unlike in most communities, the path to the Latino community's political empowerment in Central Falls was aided by the state takeover of its local schools.

Throughout the 1980s, the Central Falls School District had several challenges. Compared with other districts in the state, Central Falls had one of the lowest graduation rates, among the highest dropout rates, and among the lowest performance in math and reading proficiency. The growth of the Latino population in the city further complicated the district's challenges. By 1990, Latino students represented roughly 40 percent of the student population in Central Falls. However, there was an absence of Latino representation within the school system, particularly at the teaching and administrative levels. Additionally, the school board did not have any Latino members. Research shows that increases in Latino school board members and school administrators improve Latino parental engagement (Fraga, Meier, and England 1986; Marschall 2005; Shah 2009). The absence of a Latino presence in the school district created a fissure between the schools and the community and presented an added layer of challenges to the district, which had been struggling to meet the needs of its changing population.

In addition to the academic challenges, the city also had financial difficulties that affected the school district. Central Falls is one of the poorest cities in the state. Over 30 percent (31.7 percent) of Central Falls residents live under the poverty level, compared with 14.3 percent of the state's general population (U.S. Census 2010). By the late 1980s and early 1990s, the city, which relied on property taxes to fund its schools, had increasing difficulties funding the school system. As a result of the academic and fiscal challenges, the state of Rhode Island took over the Central Falls School District in 1991.

Following the takeover, the state abolished the all-white elected school board and created a new state-appointed board. Three out of the nine members appointed to the board were Latino. For the first time in the city's history, there was Latino representation on the school committee.

In Central Falls, the state takeover of the schools had significant political implications. For the Latino community, the takeover seemed to help establish a connection between the community and the schools, which had been largely absent prior to the takeover. Over time, the state continued to appoint Latino members to the school board, and by 2006, Latinos made up the majority of the school board. As state officials considered candidates for the Central Falls school board, descriptive representation was a key factor in their decision-making. According to Keith Oliveira, a former special assistant to the commissioner of education in Rhode Island, who was charged with recruiting candidates to the Central Falls school board, descriptive representation was an important factor. Oliveira stated:

> We knew that if we wanted to improve the schools in Central Falls, the community had to be part of it. When it came time to appoint new trustees to the school board, I wanted to make sure that we had Latinos and Latinas from Central Falls represented on the board.[11]

As Latinos transitioned into the majority on the board, there were tensions between the old guard and the new majority. One Latina school board member had the following to say about the majority-white school board prior to Latinos becoming the majority: "After the takeover, we came in, and there was a plantation mentality . . . . Those in power were the master in this plantation, and they felt like the people were grateful to get what they got. Their attitude was, 'These people don't know what they don't know.'"[12]

By the mid- to late 2000s, the majority-Latino school board had helped establish stronger links between the school district and the majority-Latino community in Central Falls. However, while the takeover helped Latinos gain greater representation on the school board, it led to a detachment between white elected officials, who still represented the majority of the power structure in Central Falls, and the school district. The mayor and city council members were not involved in any of the decision-making at the school level. During the 2005 campaign for the city's mayoralty, when asked about their vision for the school district, candidates mentioned that they had no opinion on the schools because the state controlled the school district.[13] According to one school board member, "I guess because the funding comes from the state and they don't have a say," the politicians "have distanced themselves from school issues."[14]

Despite the absence of local elected officials in school-related affairs, the school board took a leadership role in creating connections to the community. Additionally, it also took a leadership role in re-establishing ties to the city's elected officials, which had become nonexistent following the takeover. Anna Cano Morales, the chair of the Central Falls Board of Trustees, played a major role in this effort. A Central Falls native, she became chair of the board in 2006. According to Cano Morales, a social worker by training and a leader in the Latino community, she agreed to serve on the board under the condition that state officials would not undermine the board's decisions. Furthermore, she had a conversation with Commissioner Peter McWalters about her concerns with some of the board members, who, in her view, were not representative of the community. According to Cano Morales, she met with McWalters several months after her appointment to the board and said,

> Peter, I am about to have a baby. I have another baby at home, and I have a very demanding job. I am wasting my time. So I may not come back after I have my baby. And let me tell you why. Some of these men that are on the board now, they are not doing anything for the kids of Central Falls. I don't know what they are doing, but this is a disgrace. It is a joke, and I don't have any time for this.[15]

McWalters agreed with her assessment and agreed to work with her to ensure that the new appointments to the board were more reflective of the community. Within a three-year period, the board underwent a significant transformation. According to McWalters, the state could not have afforded to lose Cano Morales and the other Latina members on the board. He said, "We were beginning to work well with the community, and their departure would have hurt us."[16] By 2010, Cano Morales, along with a majority-Latina school board, which included Ana Cecilia-Rosado,

Mary Lou Perez, and Leslie Estrada, among others, had begun to make deeper inroads with the community. The emergence of the majority-Latina school board in Central Falls had political implications beyond the board itself. Similar to the case in other cities with historically marginalized populations, once the Latino community in Central Falls gained representation on the school board, the path to city council seats and the mayoralty became more accessible to them.

In 2012, the city elected James Diossa, a council member and education advocate, as the city's first Latino mayor. Unlike the previous mayor and previous mayoral candidates, Diossa made the school district a central part of his campaign. Although the state controlled the school district, Diossa focused on the schools during his campaign and stated: "City leaders have to be involved with the schools because what affects the kids is going to affect the whole city. They are our future."[17]

In addition to highlighting his work with the school district throughout the campaign, Diossa also counted on Anna Cano Morales, the school board chair, as one of his top campaign advisers. After Diossa's victory, Cano Morales also chaired Diossa's transition team. Diossa's election signified a change in the relationship among the schools, the school board, and the mayor's office. Although the state controlled the school district, Diossa also committed city resources to the district, unlike previous mayors. Furthermore, in the 2013 election, several Diossa allies, with connections to the school district, won city council seats. Among the newly elected city council members was Stephanie Gonzalez, a member of the Central Falls school board since 2011. Gonzalez maintained her seat on the school board after winning a seat on the city council, which further strengthened the connection between the school board and city government.

The emergence of the Latino leadership in Central Falls also had statewide political implications for the city and the school district. The rapid growth of the Latino population in Central Falls has garnered attention from statewide political leaders. The Latino electorate in Central Falls and the greater Providence area has strongly identified with the Democratic Party. In Rhode Island, the majority of the state political officeholders are also Democrats. The densely populated city has become an important

Democratic stronghold for Democratic candidates seeking state political office. During Diossa's inauguration as mayor of Central Falls, most state political officeholders attended the ceremony, including the city's congressional representative, the governor, the lieutenant governor, and the secretary of state, among other officials (Malinowski 2014).

In a Democratic-dominated state government, the relationship between the city's elected officials, particularly the mayor, and the governor's office and state legislature has led to stronger partnerships between state officials—who control the school district—and local political leaders. According to school board members and city leaders, the relationship is beneficial to Central Falls because it ensures better relations when school leaders visit the state house to secure funding for the district and when the school board makes decisions concerning personnel—such as hiring a superintendent of their choice—for instance.

In 2015, state leaders supported, without objection, the school board's choice to replace the retiring superintendent, Fran Gallo. Victor Capellan, a well-known education and political leader in the Latino community, was widely supported by the school board, the mayor, the community, and state officials. Following Capellan's appointment, Mayor Diossa stated that he had seen "Victor's dedication to our students firsthand and I know that our community will welcome his leadership as the next superintendent of the Central Falls School District" (Borg 2015). By 2016, the school board, the community, and the city government had undergone a transformation from isolated entities to a collaborative partnership.

The Central Falls School District still has significant challenges. As of 2016, the majority-Latino school district had persistent gaps in academic achievement compared with majority-white school districts in Rhode Island. However, in the years that the school district has established closer ties to the community, parental engagement has increased, and the dropout rate has decreased significantly as well (Harrison 2013). According to a report by the Education Alliance and the Annenberg Institute for School Reform (2013) at Brown University, between 2009 and 2012, graduation rates and scores on math proficiency exams increased.

CONCLUSION

The Newark and Central Falls cases reveal several puzzles about state take-overs and their political implications. In Newark, the takeover was hostile and had a negative effect on the city's black political empowerment. In Central Falls, the takeover helped create a path for Latinos to gain political empowerment on the school board, which leaders used to forge stronger ties to the community, elected officials in the city, and state officials. Why does state intervention affect communities differently? Additionally, in New Jersey, the Republican state administration took the lead in creating the political climate and passing the state law that allowed the state to take over local school districts. Why are Republicans—usually the champions of local control and decentralization—leading the efforts to take over local school districts? Finally, the state's role in Newark and Central Falls suggests that state administrations have the capacity to disrupt or support the local regime. What are the enduring implications of these trends for urban governance and theories of urban politics? I explore these questions in the chapters that follow. First, I begin by conducting a systematic analysis of the effects of state takeovers on black and Latino descriptive representation on local school boards.

State Takeovers and Black and Latino Political Empowerment

The previous chapter showed that takeovers had different effects on the black community in Newark, New Jersey, and the Latino community in Central Falls, Rhode Island. The Newark case supports the arguments made by communities in Baltimore, Detroit, and Oakland that takeovers are detrimental to local democracy and have a disempowering effect on local communities. However, the Central Falls case presents a puzzle because it appears that the loss of local autonomy presented an opportunity for a politically marginalized group to gain political empowerment in the city. In other words, the seemingly "undemocratic" takeover may have resulted in more equitable representation for Latinos. Moreover, the increase in participation among Latinos in the district has helped provide a climate of collaboration in the schools that has led to improved educational outcomes.

How is black and Latino representation affected by state takeovers of local government? This question is part of a larger discussion in American politics concerning decentralized and centralized government authority. In the U.S. federal system, centralization and decentralization can take different forms. However, government centralization has generally meant the concentration of governance authority at the municipal, state, or national level (Meier 2013).

The scholarship on government centralization and decentralization has generally argued in favor of decentralized arrangements as a way to enhance democratic participation (Dye 1990; Rivlin 1992). Advocates of democratic participation, dating back to Thomas Jefferson, have argued that decentralization—the closer the decision-making body is to the citizen—is the optimal arrangement for democratic participation to thrive. Scholars have also focused on how political participation and empowerment among racial minorities increase as a result of decentralized arrangements and are harmed by centralization (Chambers 2006; Fung 2004).

Although contemporary studies of centralization and its effect on political empowerment suggest that decentralized arrangements are optimal for increasing participation and empowerment, the "decentralization-as-optimal" argument ignores the complicated history that racial minorities have had with government. At times, the state has prevented racial minorities from political participation and achieving political power; and at other times, it has helped in the process of political empowerment. As Michael Dawson points out, African Americans have generally supported a strong centralized state because of the "federal government's relative support in protecting black claims for property rights and human rights against public and private expropriators in the states and local communities" (2001, 26).

Although scholars have dedicated attention to understanding the role of government intervention in addressing barriers to political participation among historically marginalized populations, the scholarship has focused on federal intervention in states and localities. We know less about how state-level intervention at the local level affects racialized communities. Historically, on issues of political empowerment and civil rights, state and local governments have been collaborators in efforts to politically marginalize racialized populations (Lowndes 2008; Mettler 1998).

As states increase their presence in local affairs, what are the political implications for communities of color? Since racial minorities have had a complex history in the struggle between local autonomy and centralized authority, when does state centralization lead to increased political empowerment for racial minorities? Conversely, when does centralized authority negatively affect political empowerment among racial minorities? The study of state takeovers of local school districts provides a useful lens to explore these questions.

To examine the effects of centralization on political empowerment, this chapter focuses on one particular aspect of political empowerment: descriptive representation. Descriptive representation has been one of the key factors that researchers have used to assess a community's level of political empowerment. Although descriptive representation is not the sole factor in helping formulate political empowerment, scholars have pointed to "its symbolic or material importance as a necessary condition or positive factor towards group empowerment" (Hardy-Fanta et al. 2005, 2). Scholars have used racial and ethnic representation in the mayor's office and on city councils as a measure of political empowerment (Browning, Marshall, and Tabb 1984; Kaufmann 2004; Owens and Brown 2013). Scholars have also demonstrated how descriptive representation can encourage political participation among racialized communities at the municipal (Bobo and Gilliam 1990; Marschall and Ruhil 2007), state (Pantoja and Segura 2003), and congressional (Tate 2003) levels. Additionally, scholars have shown that increases in descriptive representation can lead to positive policy outcomes for communities of color (Karnig and Welch 1980; Saltzstein 1989).

At the local level, the public schools have played an important role in the process of political empowerment, particularly for communities of color. Several works have shown how the schools and school boards are essential components in the schema of community political empowerment by providing a public sphere for citizen engagement (Chambers 2006; Fung 2004) and serving as a platform from which to launch battles against systemic discrimination (Katznelson and Weir 1985). Scholars have also found that increases in black and Latino descriptive representation on school boards are associated with improved student performance (Meier and England 1984; Meier and O'Toole 2006) and increases in black and Latino parental and community engagement (Fraga, Meier, and England 1986; Marschall 2005).

Finally, descriptive representation on school boards has implications for political empowerment beyond the schools. Local school boards have also been the entry point for black and Latino political officeholders. The rise of black and Latino politicians in many cities begins at the school board level. Henig et al. (2001, 34) show that blacks held seats on local school boards in major cities before gaining seats on the city council and electing the city's first black mayor. Hardy-Fanta et al. (2005) also show that Latinos serve on school boards at higher rates than in any other political office. Therefore, the literature on political empowerment, particularly among racialized communities, suggests that the conceptualization of community political empowerment should take into account the role of the public schools and descriptive representation on the school board.

Since 1989, there have been more than 100 state takeovers of local school districts in the United States. Although states execute takeovers differently, takeovers result in the shift of governance authority from local actors to state authorities (Ziebarth 2002). In addition to centralizing governance authority of the school district, state takeovers of school districts disproportionately affect black and Latino communities. Nearly 85 percent of takeovers occur in districts where blacks and Latinos make up the majority of the student population.

In most cases, takeovers result in the abolishment of the locally elected school board.[1] Some scholars have argued that takeovers violate the Voting Rights Act of 1965, by replacing elected school boards with state-appointed school boards, thereby preventing local communities from choosing their representatives (Green and Carl 2000). Researchers have also argued that the loss of decision-making authority for school boards has a negative effect on participation (Wirt and Kirst 1997). In some instances, the elected boards remain in place but are stripped of decision-making authority, leading to community concerns over decision-making power. In Oakland, for example, although the school board was not removed after the takeover in 1991, board members and community organizations still felt disempowered (Ansell, Reckhow, and Kelly 2009; Epstein 2012).

In short, the existing evidence suggests that state takeovers have a negative effect on racialized communities. However, the argument that takeovers negatively affect black and Latino political empowerment is reliant on the assumption that blacks and Latinos already have political power where the takeovers have occurred, which may not be the case even in districts where blacks and Latinos constitute a significant portion of the population. Historically, population growth has not always been a sufficient factor for black and Latino political empowerment (Morone 1990; Rocha and Matsubayashi 2013). Race and ethnicity have figured prominently in the struggle for local political power in urban politics (Browning, Marshall, and Tabb 1984; Dahl 1961; Pinderhughes 1987). Moreover, many local regimes adopt practices aimed at deliberately preventing marginalized communities from gaining power (Trounstine 2006). The relationship between black and Latino communities and the local power structure is complex, and a more complete analysis of the effects of centralization on racialized communities requires (1) a historical frame that reveals where a community is along the continuum of political power at the time of centralization and (2) a recognition that centralization may affect groups differently within the same locality.[2]

To examine the effects of state takeovers on black and Latino descriptive representation on school boards, this chapter returns to the Newark case study.[3] In terms of the size and racial and ethnic demographics of the school district, Newark is similar to the majority of the other school districts that have experienced state takeovers.[4] As in most cities that have had their school districts taken over by the state, Newark's locally elected school board was abolished, and a new board was appointed by state officials. The Newark case is also instructive because, although the state took over the Newark schools in 1995, it had initially proposed to take over the schools in the 1960s. In that period, the black and Latino communities lacked political power in the city. However, when the state took over the district in 1995, African Americans had gained significant political power in Newark, but the Latino community still had low levels of political empowerment. By examining Newark's experience with state intervention from a longer historical perspective, we are able to assess how communities perceive and respond to the prospects of centralized authority at a time when they have little political power and when they have gained

significant political power. The Newark case study will help inform expectations for how takeovers affect communities, which will then be tested
using an original data set of the universe of state takeovers between 1989
and 2013.

NEWARK, NEW JERSEY

As chapter 2 demonstrated, the schools played a pivotal role in helping
the black community gain political empowerment in Newark in the 1970s.
Following the 1967 rebellion in Newark, the Governor's Select Commission
on Civil Disorder cited the state of the schools in Newark as a central factor that led to the unrest in the city. Key among the state's and community's concerns was the lack of black representation and political influence
in school-related issues. In the late 1960s, blacks and Latinos represented
roughly 75 percent of the Newark public school population. However, the
school district only had one African American on the school board.

   To address the lack of black representation on the school board, the
commission recommended that the state take over the Newark schools.
In its view, a state takeover would have provided the opportunity to
restructure school governance to provide blacks greater opportunities
to influence school policy. The plan called for "subdistricts" that would
be "governed by boards of education, whose members must reside in the
subdistrict" (Lilley et al. 1968, 171). In other words, state officials were prepared to use their centralized authority in an attempt to give blacks control of their local schools.

   The black community, who did not have citywide political power,
viewed the potential takeover positively. Several leaders, including
Kenneth Gibson, who would become the city's first black mayor in 1970,
supported the plan (Rich 1996). Latinos, mostly of Puerto Rican descent,
were not vocal about the proposed takeover. However, the lack of Latino
representation and political power in Newark led Puerto Rican leaders to
join African Americans to form the Black and Puerto Rican Convention in
1969, which mobilized to help Gibson become the city's mayor (Woodward

1999). Since blacks and Latinos did not control the Newark schools, the state takeover would not necessarily have been detrimental to their communities.[5] On the other hand, white politicians, who still had political control of the city, opposed the takeover. Anthony Imperiale, head of the North Ward Citizens Committee, a vigilante group formed during the 1967 rebellion, who would also get elected to the Newark city council in 1969, called the state takeover plan a "governor's dictatorship" (Rich 1996).

In short, support or opposition to the proposed takeover in 1968 was based on questions of political power. The white-dominated power structure viewed the takeover as a threat and a violation of their democratic rights. On the other hand, blacks, who lacked local political power, considered the potential state takeover an opportunity to increase their political empowerment. Latinos did not oppose the takeover plan and coalesced with African Americans in an effort to increase their own political empowerment. Despite the absence of black and Latino opposition to the takeover, the state of New Jersey did not take over the Newark Public Schools in 1968.

As chapter 2 demonstrated, the state did take over the Newark schools, and African Americans felt differently about the takeover in 1995. By then, the black community had political power. The city had a black mayor and majorities on the city council and school board. As a result of the takeover, the state abolished the locally elected school board and replaced it with an advisory board. On the new state-appointed board, African Americans represented 53 percent of the board members; Latinos, 27 percent; and whites, 20 percent (Walker 1995).

The abolishment of the elected board had differing effects on the African American and Latino communities. In 1995, before the takeover, five blacks served on the nine-member elected school board, representing 56 percent of the board. When the elected body was replaced with an appointed board, black representation decreased slightly from 56 to 53 percent. For blacks, who controlled the majority of the school board before the takeover, the switch from an elected to an appointed board did not amount to a significant decrease in representation, but the takeover did result in a significant loss of substantive power. The notion of an "advisory board" had a negative effect on African Americans because prior to the takeover they had controlled the school board and had significant influence on issues related to district governance, budget, and personnel.

Latinos, on the other hand, had very little power on the school board prior to the takeover. From 1988 to 1995, there was only one Latina on the school board, although Latinos represented around 28 percent of the Newark city and student population during this period. Furthermore, in the years leading up to the takeover, there was increasing frustration among Latinos that they were not included among the decision makers in the schools. At an August 1991 school board meeting, during the public comments portion, a Latino community member stated that the "Hispanic community is displeased with the board" and indicated "that changes must be made to include Hispanic leadership."[6] At another meeting, a Latina stated "that Hispanics are not getting their fair share" when referring to the absence of Latino leadership in Newark.[7]

Therefore, the abolishment of the locally elected school board following the 1995 state takeover of the Newark schools did not represent a loss of empowerment for Latinos. In fact, Latino representation on the board increased after the takeover. Before the takeover, there was only one Latina on the nine-member elected board. After the takeover, there were four Latinos on the 15-member appointed board. The increase in Latino members raised their representation from 11 percent to 27 percent, closely resembling their overall share of the city's population.

Although the newly appointed board was only to serve in an "advisory" capacity, the Latino members of the advisory board brought forth issues of importance to the Latino community that were not raised at the board meetings prior to the takeover. An analysis of the board meeting minutes following the takeover reveals that Latino board members raised issues specifically concerning the Latino community, including concerns with bilingual education, construction bids for Latino businesses, and contracts for Latino vendors in the school district.[8] The concerns brought forth by the appointed Latino members of the school board also show that board members viewed the school district not only as an educational institution but as a vehicle to expand economic opportunity to the city's Latino community as well.

In addition to increasing Latino representation on the board, the takeover seemed to spur greater interest in school-level politics among Latinos in Newark. In 2000, the school board switched back from an appointed board to an elected board, and Latinos participated at higher rates than in the period before the takeover.[9] By 2003, Latinos had five representatives on the nine-member school board (see Figure 3.1). This marked the first time that the Newark school board had a Latino majority. Just eight years earlier, members of Newark's Latino community had raised concerns about their lack of representation in leadership positions within the school board. Furthermore, in 2004, six Latinos ran for a position on the advisory board. It was the highest number of Latino candidates in the history of Newark's school board elections.[10] Interestingly, despite the significant gains in school board representation, the Latino population in Newark had only increased from 26 percent in 1990 to 29 percent by 2000. Therefore, the increase in school-related political participation among Latinos in Newark cannot be simply attributed to their increase in population.

The findings from the Newark case study show that time and place on the spectrum of political empowerment were important factors in

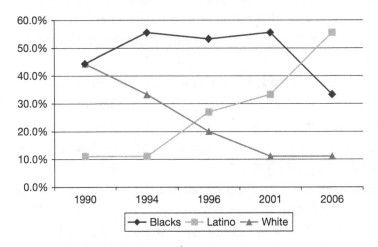

Figure 3.1. Newark School Board Descriptive Representation, 1990–2006

understanding how communities perceived and were affected by centralized government arrangements. In 1968, the city's black community
welcomed the proposed takeover of the schools because they viewed the
state's involvement as an opportunity to break through the barriers to
political empowerment imposed by the white-dominated power structure
at the time. However, by 1995, when the state did take over the Newark
schools, blacks were in control of the city and school politics and viewed
the state role as an intrusion.

Indeed, the state takeover had a negative effect on the black community. While black descriptive representation did not decrease significantly,
the symbolism of equitable representation did not have any meaningful
effect on a community that had substantive political power before the
takeover. As a result of the takeover, local black leaders were no longer
able to influence school policy or play a role in school-based employment decisions to the extent that they were able to do prior to the takeover. On the other hand, the Newark case study also suggests that the
state takeover was not detrimental to Latino political empowerment in
Newark. As a result of the takeover, Latino representation on the school
board increased. In addition, the increase in representation seemed to
have a positive effect on Latino interest in participating in school politics in the years following the takeover. Contrary to the experience of
the African American community, the findings suggest that the symbolic representation that resulted from the state takeover may have led
to increasing levels of participation among the politically weaker Latino
community.

The Newark case study helps demonstrate that centralization can affect
communities differently. To further develop and test the theory on how
centralization affects black and Latino political empowerment, I will now
turn to a quantitative analysis relying on an original data set of state takeovers of local school districts between 1989 and 2013.

When states take over local school districts, state authorities keep the
elected school board, appoint a new school board, or abolish the school
board entirely. Following the takeover of the Newark schools in 1995,
the state abolished the elected school board and appointed a new board.

In nearly 60 percent of all state takeovers of local school districts, state authorities abolish the locally elected school board. The school board is replaced by an appointed board in 41 percent of cases. In 17 percent of cases, the school board is not replaced at all.

The literature on elected versus appointed boards and their effects on descriptive representation is scant. Moreover, the existing research has focused on mayoral and superintendent appointments on the school board, not state-appointed boards. When a state takes over a local district, abolishes the existing school board, and replaces it with an appointed board, the state's governor or commissioner of education typically makes those appointments.

Since most research on appointed boards has focused on mayoral appointments, researchers have argued that the need to maintain or create successful coalitions, particularly in urban environments, has led to the "overrepresentation" of blacks and Latinos on appointed school boards. As a result, the research shows that appointed systems tend to lead to increases in black and Latino representation on school boards (Meier and England 1984; Welch and Karnig 1978). However, the research on appointed boards is not conclusive. In a study of school boards across the United States, Stewart, England, and Meier (1989) found that blacks were actually underrepresented in appointed systems.

Although the literature on appointed boards is inconclusive, and the literature on state-appointed school boards is exiguous, the Newark case is helpful in establishing expectations on state-appointed boards. Since most state takeover laws are passed under Republican gubernatorial administrations and Democrats have a strong presence in most urban localities, the argument that appointed boards result in more racially equitable representation because of a need to maintain electoral coalitions may not apply.[11] However, the state is interested in being perceived as a legitimate authority. At the time of the Newark takeover, state officials were concerned with being perceived as "colonizers," and the commissioner of education stated that he wanted to appoint a board that was representative of the community. By providing an opportunity for multiple groups, particularly marginalized groups, to be included on governing boards, states can purchase legitimacy, even if the representation is only symbolic.

In cases where the elected board remains in place after a takeover, significant change in the descriptive representation of the school board is not expected. However, in cases where the takeover results in an appointed board and then transitions to an elected board, such as the Newark case, we might expect different outcomes. In Newark, the Latino community had low levels of representation when the school board was an elected board in the years before the takeover. However, following the takeover, the state-appointed board increased Latino representation on the board. Furthermore, when the board transitioned to an elected board, the number of Latinos running for school board positions and the number of Latinos getting elected to the school board were the highest in the history of the city.

The possibility that symbolic representation may increase Latino participation is supported by the literature on descriptive representation. Scholars have shown that symbolic representation has positive psychological effects on marginalized groups, which can have a positive effect on political efficacy (Shah 2009; Tate 2001). Thus, whereas symbolic representation may not have had a positive effect on the previously empowered group (blacks), symbolic representation seems to have had a positive effect on the politically weaker group (Latinos).

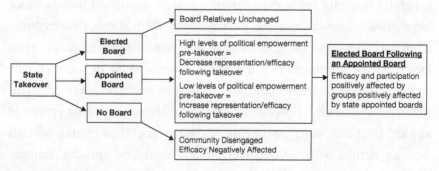

Figure 3.2. Conceptual Model of Effects of State Takeover on School Board Representation

So how do state takeovers of local school districts affect black and Latino descriptive representation? Figure 3.2 provides a diagram of the different types of school boards that are instituted by state governments following a state takeover of a local school district and how we can expect communities to be affected by each type of school board.

DATA AND MEASURES

To examine how takeovers affect black and Latino descriptive representation on local school boards, I rely on an original data set of state takeovers from 1989 to 2013.[12] I employ eight models using panel data regression with fixed effects. The panel data regression is useful for observing school districts over time. The first two models in the analysis are the baseline models. The first model uses the percentage of black school board members as the dependent variable, and the second model uses the percentage of Latino school board members as the dependent variable (see Table 3.1 for summary statistics).

Table 3.1. SUMMARY STATISTICS, DEPENDENT AND INDEPENDENT VARIABLES

Variable	Mean	SD	Minimum	Maximum
Dependent Variables				
Black Representation	0.357	0.359	0	1
Latino Representation	0.082	0.185	0	1
Independent Variables				
Black Mayor	0.297	0.457	0	1
Black City Council	0.320	0.329	0	1
Latino Mayor	0.052	0.223	0	1
Latino City Council	0.070	0.164	0	1
Population	234,377	880,506	60	8,180,000
Black % of Population	0.363	0.301	0	0.981
Latino % of Population	0.161	0.218	0	0.974

The primary explanatory variable is "Takeover," coded "0" for the period before the takeover and "1" for the period after the takeover. For data on school districts that have been taken over, including the time period of a takeover, I rely primarily on the Education Commission of the States (2004), which has a database of state takeovers between 1989 and 2004. For state takeovers after 2004, I searched for takeovers in each state that currently has a law that allows for state takeovers. As districts transition from nontakeover to takeover, I expect black and Latino descriptive representation on the school board to be affected differently according to the level of political empowerment the respective groups have at the time of the takeover.

To examine levels of black and Latino political empowerment, I include "Black Mayor" and "Latino Mayor" (0 = no; 1 = yes) and "Black City Council" and "Latino City Council" (percentage of black and Latino city council members). As levels of black and Latino political empowerment increase, as measured by mayoral and city council descriptive representation, I expect black and Latino descriptive representation on the school board to increase as well. Finally, I include a number of control variables in the models. The models include the political variable "Republican Governor" to control for the party of the governor in office at the time of the takeover. I also use the 1990, 2000, and 2010 U.S. Censuses to control for population size and black and Latino percentages of population.

In the third and fourth models, I use the same dependent variables, "Black Representation" (model 3) and "Latino Representation" (model 4), and the same independent variables used in the baseline models. However, in models 3 and 4, I include several variables to test the empowerment hypotheses. I constructed interaction terms using "Takeover" and "Black Mayor," "Black City Council," "Latino Mayor," and "Latino City Council." As black and Latino representation at the mayoral and city council levels increases, I expect the interaction with a state takeover to be negatively associated with black and Latino school board representation.

In models 5 and 6, I examine the effects of appointed boards. The models include the following variables: "Appointed" and "No School Board." I expect state-appointed boards to have a negative effect on black and

Latino descriptive representation on the school board in localities where their respective racial/ethnic group is politically empowered. Finally, in models 7 and 8, I examine the effects of elected boards. The models include "Elected," "Elected after Takeover" (school boards that remain elected following a state takeover), and "Elected after Appointed" (school boards that were initially appointed following a takeover and then transitioned to elected boards). The expectation is that black and Latino descriptive representation is not significantly affected by state takeovers when the locally elected board remains following a takeover. However, I hypothesize that black and Latino descriptive representation is positively affected when the respective group is positively affected by a state-appointed board and then the appointed board transitions to an elected board.

An analysis of the descriptive statistics shows that African Americans represented at least 50 percent of city council membership in 34 percent of pre-takeover observations. In comparison, Latino membership on city councils surpassed 50 percent in only 4 percent of pre-takeover observations. Additional analyses show that African Americans held the mayoralty in 28 percent of observations during the pre-takeover period. Latinos, on the other hand, held the mayoralty in 3 percent of observations. The results of the descriptive statistics analysis show that Latinos had low levels of political empowerment, as measured by membership on the city council and holding the mayoral seat, in the localities where takeovers occurred. In contrast, African Americans held significantly more political power in the localities where takeovers occurred. Therefore, the results of the descriptive analysis would suggest that black representation on the school board would be more negatively affected than Latino representation on the school board, if the proposed hypotheses are confirmed.

An analysis of the descriptive statistics also shows that the type of school board that states put in place following a takeover varies significantly by race and ethnicity. In 46 percent of all cases where a majority-Latino student district has been taken over, the school board remains elected, compared with only 24 percent in majority-black districts (see Figure 3.3). In takeover districts where white students represent the majority of the student population, the board remains elected in 70 percent of cases.

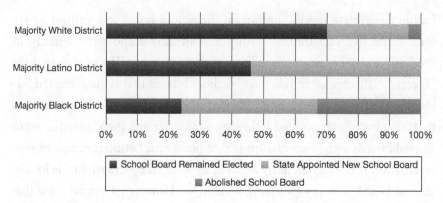

Figure 3.3. School Board Type after State Takeover of Local School District

Furthermore, in 33 percent of cases where a majority-black school district has been taken over, the school board is abolished and not replaced at all, compared with 4 percent for majority-white districts and 0 percent for majority-Latino districts. The practice of abolishing school boards following a takeover, thus, is disproportionately affecting black communities.

RESULTS

The results from the first baseline model (Black Representation) show, as expected, that increases in levels of black political empowerment are associated with increases in black representation on the school board (Black Mayor: $b = 0.06$; SE $= 0.022$; $p = .01$; and Black City Council: $b = 0.11$; SE $= 0.052$; $p = .05$) (see Table 3.2). However, as districts transition from nontakeover to takeover, black descriptive representation on the school board decreases by four percentage points ($b = -0.04$; SE $= 0.014$; $p = .01$). In contrast to the Black Representation model, the results from the Latino Representation model suggest that state takeovers of local school districts have a positive effect on Latino descriptive representation. As districts transition from nontakeover to takeover, Latino descriptive representation on the school board increases ($b = 0.02$; SE $= 0.008$; $p = .05$). Similar to the case in the Black Representation model, increases in Latino political empowerment (Latino Mayor: $b = 0.05$; SE $= 0.023$; $p = .05$; and Latino

Table 3.2. Effects of State Takeovers on Black and Latino School Board Descriptive Representation

Variable	Black Representation Baseline Model 1	Latino Representation Baseline Model 2	Black Representation Model 3	Latino Representation Model 4	Black Representation Appointed Model 5	Latino Representation Appointed Model 6	Black Representation Elected Model 7	Latino Representation Elected Model 8
Takeover	−0.042*** (0.014)	0.017** (0.008)	—	—	—	—	—	—
Black Mayor	0.061*** (0.022)	−0.002 (0.012)	0.070** (0.030)	−0.003 (0.012)	0.063*** (0.021)	−0.002 (0.012)	0.064*** (0.022)	−0.003 (0.012)
% Black City Council	0.110** (0.052)	−0.010 (0.028)	0.176*** (0.063)	−0.002 (0.028)	0.137*** (0.051)	−0.001 (0.028)	0.059 (0.052)	−0.009 (0.028)
Latino Mayor	0.034 (0.042)	0.052** (0.023)	0.031 (0.042)	0.013 (0.038)	0.030 (0.041)	0.052** (0.022)	0.030 (0.042)	0.048** (0.022)
% Latino City Council	0.018 (0.078)	0.420*** (0.042)	0.013 (0.078)	0.335*** (0.058)	−0.001 (0.077)	0.427*** (0.042)	−0.030 (0.079)	0.413*** (0.042)
Republican Governor	0.001 (0.012)	0.005 (0.006)	0.001 (0.012)	0.004 (0.006)	0.001 (0.011)	0.002 (0.006)	0.007 (0.012)	.003 (0.006)
Population	−9.85 (1.58)	−3.40 (8.61)	−1.56 (1.58)	−4.35 (8.55)	−5.00 (1.56)	−2.97 (8.65)	−1.01 (1.59)	−1.54 (8.63)
Black % of Population	0.610*** (.158)	0.042 (0.085)	0.582*** (0.157)	0.045 (0.085)	0.644*** (0.155)	0.047 (0.083)	0.590*** (0.158)	0.061 (0.085)
Latino % of Population	0.275** (0.131)	0.328*** (0.071)	0.238* (0.131)	0.325*** (0.069)	0.211* (0.126)	0.364*** (0.039)	0.193 (0.129)	0.350*** (0.070)
Black Mayor × Takeover	—	—	−0.027 (0.037)	—	—	—	—	
Black City Council Seats × Takeover	—	—	−0.098** (0.047)	—	—	—	—	
Latino Mayor × Takeover	—	—	—	0.060 (0.045)	—	—	—	

(continued)

Table 3.2. (CONTINUED)

Variable	Black Representation Baseline Model 1	Latino Representation Baseline Model 2	Black Representation Model 3	Latino Representation Model 4	Black Representation Appointed Model 5	Latino Representation Appointed Model 6	Black Representation Elected Model 7	Latino Representation Elected Model 8
Latino City Council Seats × Takeover	—	—	—	0.137** (0.057)	—	—	—	—
Appointment	—	—	—	—	−0.050** (0.020)	0.008 (0.011)	—	—
No School Board	—	—	—	—	−0.231*** (0.036)	−0.004 (0.020)	—	—
Elected	—	—	—	—	—	—	0.053*** (0.016)	0.011 (0.008)
Elected after Takeover	—	—	—	—	—	—	0.007 (0.019)	0.015 (0.010)
Elected after Appointed	—	—	—	—	—	—	0.057 (0.036)	0.035* (0.019)
Constant	0.075 (0.071)	−0.018 (.038)	0.081 (0.071)	−0.011 (0.038)	0.049 (0.070)	−0.023 (0.039)	0.045 (0.072)	−0.038 (0.039)
R^2	0.499	0.660	0.420	0.623	0.574	0.668	0.482	0.684
Observations	844	844	844	844	844	844	844	844
Number of Groups	94	94	94	94	94	94	94	94

NOTE: Panel data regression model with fixed effects.

*$p < .10$, **$p < .05$, ***$p < .01$.

City Council: $b = 0.42$; SE = 0.043; $p = .001$) are associated with increases in Latino representation on the school board.

In the third and fourth models, I include interaction terms to test the empowerment hypotheses. The results from the third model (Black Representation) show that when "Black Mayor" and "Black City Council Seats" interact with "Takeover," increases in black political empowerment are negatively associated with black representation on the school board following a takeover. Although both interaction terms suggest a negative association, only the Black City Council interaction reaches conventional levels of statistical significance ($b = -0.098$; SE = 0.047; $p = .04$). The findings suggest that cities with high levels of black membership on city councils are associated with a 10 percent decrease in black school board membership following a state takeover.

In cities that had large black city council majorities prior to the state takeover of the local schools, such as Baltimore, Detroit, Newark, and New Orleans, whose school boards averaged 10 seats prior to the takeover, the 10 percent decrease in black school board membership resulted in the loss of one black school board member. The loss of a black school board member has implications for community representation on the board. Additionally, the loss of a school board seat can have implications for black majorities on the school board as well as the potential disruption of school board coalitions.

Unlike the Black Representation model, the interaction terms in the Latino Representation model (fourth model), "Latino Mayor × Takeover" and "Latino City Council Seats × Takeover," are positively associated with Latino school board representation following a takeover. Although both interaction terms are positively associated with Latino school board representation, only "Latino City Council Seats × Takeover" reaches conventional levels of statistical significance ($b = 0.14$; SE = 0.057; $p = .02$). The results of the empowerment hypotheses models suggest that increases in black political empowerment are negatively associated with black school board representation following a takeover but increases in Latino political empowerment are positively associated with Latino school board representation following a takeover. However, the lack of variation as a result of

the very low levels of Latino representation on city councils and low numbers of Latino mayors in the observed districts in the pre-takeover period
should be taken into account when interpreting these results.

In models 5 and 6, I test the appointed boards hypotheses and include
"Appointment" and "No School Board" as independent variables in the
models. The results show that state-appointed school boards following
a state takeover are negatively associated with black school board representation. In districts where a takeover results in an appointed school
board, black representation decreases by 5 percent following the takeover
($b = -0.05$; SE = 0.020; $p = .05$). The results also show that when school
boards are abolished and not replaced at all, black representation is significantly negatively affected ($b = -0.23$; SE = 0.032; $p = .001$). These findings suggest that when states take over a local school district and replace
the school board with an appointed board or abolish it altogether, black
representation on the school board is negatively affected.

In model 6, the Latino Representation model, the "Appointment" variable, unlike in the Black Representation model, is positively associated with
Latino representation, although the effect does not obtain conventional
levels of statistical significance. Similarly, the "No School Board" variable
is not statistically significant, although the variable is negatively associated
with Latino descriptive representation on the school board.

Finally, in models 7 and 8, I test the elected boards hypotheses. The
findings show that elected boards, during the pre- and post-takeover periods, are positively associated with black school board representation. The
findings suggest that when school boards remain elected following a takeover, black school board representation is not negatively affected by the
state takeover. Interestingly, in the Latino Representation model, the only
statistically significant variable is the "Elected after Appointed" variable.
That is, following a takeover, boards that were initially appointed and then
transitioned to elected are positively associated with Latino school board
representation ($b = 0.04$; SE = 0.019). Similar to the findings in the Newark
case study, Latino representation on the school board seems to be positively affected when the school board transitions from an appointed board
to an elected board following a takeover.

CONCLUSION

Research has had little to say about the political implications of state centralization and state takeovers, particularly for communities of color. Furthermore, to the extent that the existing research is informative, it suggests that a state takeover is unequivocally disempowering to local communities. In this study, I propose a framework that suggests that centralization affects communities differently, depending on the level of political empowerment a community has at the time of centralization.

This chapter examined the effects of centralization on racialized communities by exploring how state takeovers of local school districts affect black and Latino descriptive representation on local school boards. Relying on a case study of Newark, New Jersey, and analysis of the universe of state takeovers between 1989 and 2013, I find support for the argument that the effects of takeovers are influenced by the level of political empowerment a particular community has at the time of the takeover. The findings show that state intervention has the capacity to address political marginalization at the local level by creating opportunities for previously excluded groups to participate in governance decisions.

In 1968, the black and Latino communities in Newark, who were politically marginalized, did not oppose a state plan to take over the school district, because they viewed the proposed intervention as a potential path to political empowerment. However, in 1995, when the state took over the Newark schools, blacks had political power and viewed the takeover as a threat to their political empowerment. Latinos, on the other hand, who had low levels of political empowerment at the time of the takeover, did not view the takeover as a threat and, in fact, gained greater representation on the school board as a result of the takeover. Moreover, the findings from this study suggest that the symbolic representation of a previously marginalized group can lead to greater efficacy and political participation on the part of that group.

These findings are consistent with the experience of the Latino community in Central Falls, Rhode Island, following the state takeover of the local schools. Research has also shown a similar effect on the Latino community in the city of Lawrence, Massachusetts, when it experienced a state takeover of the local school district. Like Central Falls, Lawrence is a majority-Latino school district, and in a study of the Lawrence takeover, Schueler (2016) finds that since Latinos had low levels of political empowerment in the school district, the takeover was not perceived as a hostile intervention that threatened the community's political power. Therefore, the findings from this study suggest that state governments can assume a role, which has traditionally been relegated to the federal government, of addressing racial inequities at the local level.

However, despite the state's potential to address political marginalization at the local level, the results of this study also show that state takeovers can have a detrimental effect on local communities. The results of the analysis show that state takeovers mostly occur in majority-black school districts. Moreover, the results also show that state takeovers most negatively affect black communities, the group with the highest levels of political empowerment in most districts that experienced state takeovers. The abolishment of locally elected school boards following a takeover disproportionately affected black communities. The practice of abolishing a locally elected school board and not replacing the board at all has primarily affected black communities. By comparison, although white communities are less likely to experience a state takeover of their local school districts, in cases where majority-white school districts were taken over, the state takeover of the local school district did not result in the abolishment of the locally elected school board. In sum, black communities are more likely than white communities to experience the political disruption that is caused by the abolishment of locally elected school boards following a takeover.

Since the research has shown that school boards are an important part of the local political ecosystem, the findings from this chapter, which demonstrate that state takeovers disrupt local school political dynamics, provoke further questions about state takeovers of local school districts. Key among them is the effect of takeovers on black communities. The fact that black communities have been disproportionately negatively affected by state takeovers of local school districts suggests that in addition to examining the effects of state interventions, the logic, justification, and intentions of state centralization should be explored as well. In the next chapter, we examine the reasons for a state takeover.

Why Take Over?

*State Centralization and the
Conservative Education Logic*

The empirical results in chapter 3 show that state intervention has the capacity to address political marginalization at the local level by creating opportunities for previously excluded groups to participate in governance decisions. However, despite the potential to address political marginalization at the local level, the findings also showed that state takeovers could have a detrimental effect on local communities. Black communities in particular—the communities with the highest levels of political empowerment in cities that experienced state takeovers—were most negatively affected by takeovers.

Why do state takeovers disproportionately affect black communities? Additionally, why do black communities disproportionally experience the most punitive forms of state takeovers? As chapter 3 demonstrated, when states take over local school districts, state authorities adopt one of three possible options: (1) keep the elected school board, (2) abolish the locally elected board and appoint a new school board, or (3) abolish the locally elected school board and not replace it at all. The abolishment of locally elected school boards following a takeover has disproportionately affected black communities. Although majority-white communities are less likely to experience a state takeover of their local school districts, in cases where majority-white school districts were taken over, the takeovers rarely result in the abolishment of the locally elected school board. To understand why state takeovers disproportionately affect black communities, we have to understand why states take over school districts in the first place.

JUSTIFYING STATE TAKEOVERS

Proponents of state takeovers have argued that takeovers are necessary to improve low-performing school districts. In Michigan, the governor and state legislature cited low academic achievement in the Detroit schools to introduce and enact the takeover law that was used to take over the school district in 1999 (Mirel 2004). Similarly, New Jersey's State Board of Education argued that Newark students deserved the constitutional right to an "adequate education" to justify the takeover of the Newark schools in 1995 (Reilly 1995). In 2015, the Georgia state legislature approved a measure to place a referendum on a statewide ballot to give the governor authority to take over school districts. The language on the ballot read: "Shall the Constitution of Georgia be amended to allow the state to intervene in chronically failing public schools in order to improve student performance?" (Bluestein and Hallerman 2016).

Although state officials and supporters of state takeovers have relied on a rhetoric of academic achievement to justify takeovers of local school districts, poor academic performance does not fully explain why states adopted takeovers as a policy option. Americans have always had concerns about the state of education in the United States. In the late 18th century, educators "lamented the conditions of American schools" (Kaestle 1983, 8). In the 19th century, political opponents challenged efforts to create a public education system. In the 1950s, President Eisenhower raised concerns about American education and connected the concerns to matters of national security. In 1983, President Reagan's National Commission on Excellence in Education published *A Nation at Risk* with the aim of bringing attention to education concerns in the United States. The commission wrote,

We report to the American people that while we can take justifiable pride in what our schools and colleges have historically accomplished and contributed to the United States and the well-being of its people, the educational foundations of our society are presently being eroded by a rising tide of mediocrity that threatens our very future as a Nation and a people. (National Commission on Excellence in Education 1983, 7)

Thus, concerns with low academic performance alone do not explain why states began to take over local school districts in the late 1980s and 1990s. Moreover, low academic performance does not explain why black communities are more likely to experience the most punitive form of state takeover. In West Virginia and Kentucky, for instance, where several majority-white school districts have been taken over by the state, state officials left the elected board in place. In Mississippi, on the other hand, where the majority of state takeovers have occurred in majority-black communities, takeovers have resulted in the complete abolishment of the local school board.

The abolishing of the local school board and the turmoil that it has led to in many communities is puzzling from an education perspective. Education scholars have shown that schools perform better when there is a collaborative working environment among educators, administrators, and communities (Hong 2011; Noguera 2003; Warren and Mapp 2011). Similarly, political scientists have argued that sustainable school improvement efforts are most successful when "civic capacity"—community stakeholders working together—is established in school communities (Henig et al. 2001; Shipps 2003; Stone 2001).

In his book on successful school reform in Union City, New Jersey, a mostly Latino immigrant community across the Hudson River from New York City, David Kirp (2013) notes how the community, school officials, and local political leaders were able to work collectively to improve education in the city. Interestingly, the state threatened to take over the Union City school district in the early 1990s, but by the mid-1990s, state officials decided not to take over the district. Today, Union City is considered a model of successful urban school district reform.

Thus, the education and political science research points to models of collaboration between community stakeholders as a necessary ingredient to successful school improvement. However, despite the body of evidence that shows that school districts are more likely to improve education outcomes when there is collaboration between key stakeholders, including state officials, why would states pursue policies that lead to political disruption and hostility between local communities and state government? Based on what we know about education, the evidence on successful school reform does not support justifying a hostile takeover of a local school district because it might lead to improved educational outcomes.

In this chapter, I will argue that there are political and economic reasons that help explain why states take over local school districts. More specifically, the chapter will argue that race politics has been a major factor in the emergence of state takeovers. In the pages that follow, I will show that state takeovers fit into a broader historical narrative of state centralization. States did not always have the interest or capacity to take over school districts. However, by the 1970s, several factors led states to centralize governance authority and increase their presence in local affairs. Most notably, I will argue, the political tumult of the 1960s had a significant effect on the rise of state power and the emergence of state takeovers. In other words, state takeovers emerged as a response to the political changes of the 1960s and the rise of black political empowerment in U.S. cities. By viewing takeovers from a political, not simply an education, perspective, we can better explain why state takeovers disproportionately affect black communities.

The first part of this chapter will focus on examining the factors that led to the rise of state centralization and state takeovers as a policy option. That will be followed by an analysis of a sample of nearly 1,000 school districts to assess the factors that are associated with the likelihood of a takeover. The results of the analysis will show that there is a correlation among black political power in cities, state and federal resources for local education, and state takeovers of local school districts.

STATE CENTRALIZATION

As previous chapters have shown, state takeovers of local school districts emerged in the late 1980s. In 1988, New Jersey passed the first state takeover law, and by the year 2000, 13 additional states had passed state takeover laws as well. State governments did not always have the interest or the capacity to take over local school districts. However, in the 1970s several factors contributed to the rise of greater state centralization, which provided states the capacity *and* motives to take over local school districts.

In the early 1900s, state governments played an important role in the Progressives' efforts to reform government. In that same period, state governments had developed an increasing interest in local school districts as well. However, limits on state capacity prevented states from intervening in local schools in significant ways (Manna 2006; Murphy 1973; Timar 1997). Even in cases where certain states had more capacity to intervene than weaker states, as Tracy Steffes (2012) notes, "ideological commitments" in addition to political realities and respect for local control meant that state involvement in local schools was subtle and looked more like partnerships, rather than imposing interventions from state officials. Yet, despite the significance of state governments for reformers in the early 1900s, by the 1930s, the New Deal "order" ushered in an era of an activist national government that weakened state powers (Weier 2005). However, in the 1960s, several factors began to emerge that ultimately swung the pendulum in the favor of state governments.

The first was the increasing capacity of state governments. In the 1960s, grants from the federal government sent to the states to address specific issues of education, poverty, and infrastructure, among other issues, helped states build capacity and expand their governmental reach in ways that were previously unfeasible (Hanson 1998; Hedge 1998; Manna 2006). In addition to gaining greater capacity, states also gained greater powers. By the early 1970s, the Nixon administration's "New Federalism" devolved decision-making powers to the states (Conlan 1998; Nice 1998; Reagan 1972). Under this new policy, programs that had previously fallen within the purview of the federal government were now under the authority of the states. In the 1980s, President Reagan expanded on Nixon's "New Federalism."

Changes at the local level also helped expand the powers of state governments. At the same time that states gained greater authority, local governments began to become increasingly dependent on state governments (Agranoff and McGuire 1998). Deindustrialization and population declines contributed to eroding tax bases for urban localities. For instance, in the early 1900s, 95 percent of local government revenue was generated locally. By the late 20th century, local governments received one-third of their revenue from the state and national governments (Nice 1998).

The combination of greater state capacity, the devolution of authority from the federal government to the states under the Nixon and Reagan administrations, and the decline in local resources contributed to the increasing powers of states, which allowed states to enlarge their presence in local affairs. In addition to these factors, race—a factor that has received considerably less attention from scholars—has also greatly influenced the conditions that have led to greater state centralization.

RACE POLITICS AND THE RISE OF STATE CENTRALIZATION

In *Rise of the States*, Jon Teaford (2002) argues that the rise of state prominence after the 1960s was a "culmination of decades of change," which included the professionalization of state governments in addition to decades-long efforts by state governments to centralize authority. Teaford also notes that the rise of state centralization in the 1960s and 1970s came at a time when scholars had predicted that a "federal-urban axis"—an alliance between the national government and the cities that promised to further weaken state governments—was beginning to emerge (2002, 3). Although Teaford credits the growth of state powers to professionalization and changes that had been decades in the making, race politics also influenced the great expansion of state powers in the 1970s.

First, the declines in local tax bases, which led cities to depend more on state governments, were partly driven by segregation and "white flight" from cities (Sugrue 1996). By the middle of the 20th century, whites were leaving cities, which had significant economic implications for U.S. cities. In 1967, President Lyndon Johnson established the Kerner Commission to examine the factors that had led to racial tensions in cities across the United States throughout the mid-1960s. The Kerner Report concluded that segregation and discrimination were major contributing factors in a nation that was "moving toward two societies, one black, one white— separate and unequal" (National Advisory Commission on Civil Disorders 1968, 1).

Second, by the late 1960s and early 1970s, the "federal-urban axis" had adopted a pro–civil rights agenda that was problematic for conservatives and anti–civil rights forces. As Pierson and Skocpol note, an activist federal government in the 1960s and early 1970s led to "federal activism on behalf of citizen rights" (2007, 3), which led conservatives to mobilize against the liberal "sway" in Washington. While Pierson and Skocpol note the countermobilization among conservatives at the national level, the effects of federal activism had significant political consequences at the local level. President Johnson's Great Society programs, particularly the antipoverty programs, were a deliberate effort by the national government to provide resources and services to predominantly black communities in cities. President Johnson named his effort to connect leadership at the national level to the leaders at the community level "creative federalism" (Krasovic 2016, 3). In addition to sending resources from the national government to cities, the antipoverty programs, which included the Community Action Program, also created avenues for black political mobilization.

The Community Action Program was created in 1964 under the Economic Opportunity Act. The purpose of the program was to allow community action agencies in cities across the country to develop their own plans to "alleviate poverty" (Greenstone and Peterson 1973). In an effort to ensure that the poor and the marginalized participated in the antipoverty programs, the Economic Opportunity Act required "maximum feasible participation" by the poor. According to Daniel Moynihan, one of the architects of the Economic Opportunity Act, the phrase "maximum feasible participation" was intended to "ensure that persons excluded from the political process in the South and elsewhere would nonetheless participate in the benefits of the community action programs of the new legislation" (1969, 87). The concern was that the "local white power structure would control the allocation of community action money" without including blacks in the process (1969, 87).

Although the idea of "maximum feasible participation" was primarily created with the anticipation of southern resistance in mind, the participation requirement, along with the Community Action Program, had a significant effect in cities throughout the North as well (Krasovic 2016; Morone 1990; Rabig 2016). In cities such as New York, Chicago, Detroit, and Newark, black participation in the Community Action Program "set off local political struggles which crystallized and dramatized changing alignments in American politics" (Greenstone and Peterson 1973, 2).

For conservatives and anti–civil rights forces, black political mobilization in cities—in the North as well as the South—was a major concern. In addition to opposing antipoverty programs based on fiscal concerns, conservatives viewed black mobilization as a political threat as well. By the 1960s, African Americans had become a major part of the Democratic coalition, while social and fiscal conservatives consolidated within the Republican coalition. Therefore, the federal-urban axis that emerged in the 1960s, which embraced a pro–civil rights agenda, presented political challenges for conservatives.

The political response to the federal-urban axis by conservatives was to strengthen state governments. The Nixon and Reagan administrations' efforts to dismantle the funding streams from the federal government directly to cities were aimed at disrupting the federal-urban axis that had developed by the late 1960s. Both Nixon and Reagan considered community development programs, particularly the Community Action Program, a political threat because they served to mobilize communities of color (Conlan 1998; Kantor 1988). From 1955 to 1975 federal aid that went directly to cities, bypassing states, increased by over 4,000 percent (Kantor 1988, 214). However, in the mid-1980s, the Reagan administration cut funds for community development by nearly 40 percent, representing the largest cuts in funding by the administration (Conlan 1998, 148). By disrupting the pipeline between the federal government and cities, Nixon and Reagan strengthened the role of states. Thus, the era of "New Federalism," which has typically been considered an era of devolution, also ushered in an era of centralization—where states would gain greater say over local governance.

Finally, the emergence of black-led urban political regimes helped remove an enduring obstacle to state centralization.[1] By the late 1960s and early 1970s, capacity was no longer the obstacle that it had previously been for state governments in their efforts to centralize authority. However, the American political tradition of local control had provided a check on state centralization. Throughout the 20th century, concern over government power prevented state governments from expanding their reach into localities. Scholars of U.S. political development accurately point to America's "liberal tradition" and its embrace of limited government to explain American resistance to the expansion of state powers (Hartz 1955).

However, by the 1970s and early 1980s, blacks had gained majorities on school boards and city councils as well as mayoralties in many U.S. cities (Colburn 2001; Nelson and Meranto 1977). The emergence of black political leadership at the local level presented a challenge for conservatives, who had traditionally championed decentralization and local democracy but were unwilling to devolve power to communities that represented the political opposition. Conservatives capitalized on white racial resentment and fear of black political mobilization and black political control of cities to justify an expansion of state authority. Although conservative ideology and principles espoused small government and favored decentralization and strong local democracy, demands by black communities, and other communities of color, for greater local control were met with resistance. Republican powerbrokers jettisoned the conservative principles of local democracy in favor of centralized state government and disrupting the federal-urban axis.

Thus, the emergence of black-led urban regimes eliminated the final hurdle to centralization. By the 1970s, states had the capacity *and* the license to centralize authority.[2] Fiscal concerns, black mobilization at the local level, and the emergence of black political leadership at the city level provided the optimal set of justifications for conservatives to centralize authority at the state level. Moreover, by the 1970s, the conservative movement at the state level also led to, and was aided by, the emergence of influential policy organizations including the Heritage Foundation (1973), the American Legislative Exchange Council (ALEC) (1973), and Cato Institute (1977) (Mayer 2016). These organizations helped shape the conservative agenda, which included centralization of state power in the 1970s.

Perhaps more so than any other policy domain, control over public education became a central point of contention between state and urban localities. School politics was a source of political mobilization for black communities. School politics paved the path to black political empowerment in cities. Moreover, starting in the 1970s, black teachers became an increasingly important aspect of the black political apparatus in U.S. cities (Orr 1999). By the 1980s and 1990s, black teachers represented the majority of teachers in cities such as Baltimore, Newark, and New Orleans (Carr 2014; Orr 1999). As black communities increasingly mobilized, they also demanded greater resources for local school systems that had been negligent to black students.

Finally, as federal legislation and court decisions began to dismantle legal forms of disenfranchisement, the concentration of black populations in heavily populated urban centers meant that as blacks gained greater political power in cities, they also became an increasingly important constituency in state politics. Thus, the improvement of education for black children was inextricably linked to the political success of the black community. Conservatives, who by the 1960s and 1970s began identifying overwhelmingly with the Republican Party, professed the need to improve education for black students while at the same time undermining the political empowerment of the black community.

This *conservative education logic* is problematic for many reasons. The attempt to separate black political power from the process of educating black children raises important education and political questions, which I will discuss in greater detail in chapter 6. The logic of separating black political empowerment from the process of educating black children also raises questions about urban governance, particularly how the increasing presence of state governments in localities affects black-led urban regimes. I will explore this question in greater detail in chapter 5. At a minimum, however, the attempt to separate black political power from the process of educating black children helps explain why contestation and hostility between state governments and black communities have prevailed over collaboration.

Additionally, the *conservative education logic* also provides an alternative explanation for the expanding role of governors in education. In the 1960s and 1970s, a number of governors from southern states began expanding their presence in education (Henig 2013). The emergence of "education governors" began in the South. Scholars often attribute the expanding role of governors in education to the significance of education in a state's economic development agenda (Henig 2013; Herrington and Fowler 2003; Vinovskis 2008). Indeed, governors are responsible for setting an economic agenda for their respective states, and education, which by the 1980s had become the largest item on state budgets, was a central part of states' economic policies.

Yet the focus on economic interests while ignoring political interests fails to provide a more complete explanation of the role of governors, particularly southern governors, in education beginning in the 1960s. Jeffrey Henig acknowledges the role of race and politics to offer an explanation for why southern governors were among the first to engage in school politics in the 1960s and 1970s. Henig argues that after years of being viewed as obstructionists in the pursuit of educational opportunities, southern governors were able to take a leadership role in education "after the South dropped its massive resistance" and "after real progress had begun to be made in dismantling dual education systems" (2013, 74). Thus, southern governors, who had an interest in intervening in education for economic reasons, saw their opportunity to exert their presence once the South was no longer seen as a hindrance to educational opportunity.

However, since education has been used as a tool for economic and political development, the view that southern governors in the 1960s and

1970s deviated from the obstructionist posture of the 1950s would suggest that southern governors were committed to the political development of black communities in the South. The evidence on southern governors is not supportive of this perspective, and in fact, the rich literature on south-ern politics in the 1960s points to the subtle and "raging" resistance to black political rights by citizens and their elected officials, including governors (Bartley and Graham 1975; Black 1976; D. Carter 1995; McMillen 1971).

Instead, the rise of "education governors" in the South should be seen as an attempt to curtail the potential effects of black political prog-ress emanating from cities in the 1960s. The civil rights movement and demands for better educational opportunities for black children began to challenge existing political dynamics in the South. Additionally, by the 1960s, Supreme Court rulings on district apportionments had led to the increasing political significance of urban centers in the South (Kapeluck, Steed, and Moreland 2006).

This alternative view suggests that the South never dropped its resist-ance to the political empowerment of black communities but, rather, strengthened the role of governors as a way to disrupt the federal-urban axis that began to emerge in the 1960s. From this perspective, governors became a bulwark against the expansion of black empowerment and assumed the mantle in reshaping a resistance to black citizenship that has been reproduced throughout U.S. history following periods of democratic expansion for racialized communities. Thus, the presence of governors in education was both an economic and political imperative.

By the 1980s, the office of the governor had emerged as a powerful force in American politics. As their powers grew, governors increased their role in local public education and "claimed authority that they had previously been content to leave in the hands of state boards of education and state superintendents" (McDermott 2011, 59). As a sign of the increasing role of governors in education policy, in 1985, Lamar Alexander, the Republican governor of Tennessee, became chair of the National Governors Association. Alexander, who was known as the "Education Governor," made education a top priority for the National Governors Association (McDermott 2011).

The push to pass laws that allowed state governments to take over school districts was led by governors. At the 1986 annual meeting of the National Governors Association, the governors announced a plan that would be part of a "second wave of reform in American public education" and introduced the policy of "state takeovers of districts that failed to meet toughened minimum standards."[3] Governors from northern states joined governors from the South in the mobilization efforts to reshape education. Thomas Kean, the Republican governor of New Jersey, stated, "Education is now good politics," and added that governors "have a responsibility to massively intervene and make sure those schools do educate our children" (Herbes 1986, 1).

In addition to being an initiative led by governors, the push to pass state takeover laws had an associated partisan element. Efforts to allow states to take over school districts were led primarily by Republican governors. Eighty percent of all takeover laws in the United States were passed under Republican gubernatorial administrations. In chapter 5, I examine how partisan dynamics shaped the politics in New Jersey's efforts to take over the Newark Public Schools; the partisan element in New Jersey and the other states that passed state takeover laws suggests that takeovers are in part motivated by partisan dynamics.

By the mid-1980s, education had become "good politics" for governors. Governors had the incentives, momentum, and political tools to intervene in the public schools in unprecedented ways. In 1986, Governor Kean introduced legislation in New Jersey to allow the state to take over local school districts. In 1988, the state legislature approved the measure. New Jersey's state takeover law was the first in the nation, and by the end of the 1990s, 13 additional states had laws that allowed their respective governments to take over their local school districts (see Figure 4.1; Herbes 1986).

The expansion of state takeover laws seems to be consistent with the trajectory of other education policy initiatives in the United States, transitioning from policy innovation—a policy that is new to a state—to adoption in other states (Berry and Berry 1990; Crain 1966; Gray 1973; Shipan and Volden 2008; Walker 1969). In the United States, the absence of a centralized education policy decision body means that the process of policy

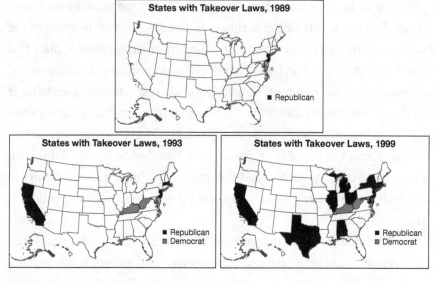

Figure 4.1. State Takeover Laws by State, 1989–1999

diffusion, where states are influenced by decisions made in other states, plays an important role in education policy (Manna 2006; Mintrom and Vergari 1998). For instance, scholars have shown how policy diffusion influenced the adoption of school choice policies (Mintrom 1997) and the expansion of charter school legislation (Wong and Langevin 2005).

Between 1988 and 2000, 14 states passed state takeover laws. This takeover incubation period was pivotal because the majority (67 percent) of all state takeovers of local school districts have happened in states that passed laws during this period. Although policy diffusion may help explain how state takeover laws began in New Jersey and then expanded to other states, the justification to pass state takeover laws based on the argument that takeovers would lead to better educational outcomes is not as clear. The research on state takeovers and their effects on academic performance between 1990 and 2000 suggested that takeovers did not have a significant effect on school improvement.[4] Despite an absence of evidence that takeovers led to better school outcomes during this important incubation period, states continued to pass state takeover laws, which suggests that there was a benefit to the policy other than just academic performance outcomes. Questions concerning resources for education factored into the emergence of state takeover laws as well.

THE COURTS AND EDUCATION RESOURCES
FOR LOCALITIES

In 1968, parents in San Antonio filed a federal lawsuit against the state of Texas, claiming that the state's system of funding the schools was inequitable and violated the equal protection clause of the Fourteenth Amendment. Demetrio Rodriguez and six other plaintiffs argued that the disparities in school funding across the district disadvantaged the lower-resourced communities in San Antonio and other cities across the state. In 1971, the U.S. District Court for the Western District of Texas ruled in favor of the plaintiffs, arguing that school funding in Texas did violate the equal protection clause in the Constitution. Following the court's ruling, the state of Texas appealed the decision, and the Supreme Court, citing probable jurisdiction, agreed to hear the case (Ogletree 2014).

In 1973, the Supreme Court decided against the plaintiffs in *San Antonio School District v. Rodriguez* and ruled that the right to an education is not protected under the Fourteenth Amendment. The decision closed the door to school finance litigation challenges at the federal level. However, the Court's decision led to a movement of state-based challenges to school financing systems. As Douglas Reed has noted the Supreme Court's decision "left an opening for state courts and state constitutions, an opportunity that school finance equity activists were quick to exploit" (2001, 9). In the 1970s, communities began challenging education funding disparities in the state courts.

The first successful school funding challenge came in 1973, in *Robinson v. Cahill*, when a New Jersey state court decided in favor of plaintiffs seeking to increase school funding for low-resource communities in the state (Yaffe 2007). Then in 1985, the state Supreme Court agreed with plaintiffs who argued that *Robinson v. Cahill* did not go far enough in addressing school funding inequities in low-resource communities and issued the first ruling in the *Abbott v. Burke* case. In New Jersey and other states where plaintiffs won school funding litigation, wealthy communities and their mostly nonurban state legislators responded negatively to the state court decisions and opposed raising state taxes to increase funding for low-resourced communities.

As the Newark case demonstrated, nonurban state legislators vehemently opposed raising taxes to support education in low-resourced school districts. In New Jersey, the successful effort to bring additional resources for education into urban districts was also accompanied by a state monitoring regime that led to the takeover of the local schools. In addition to opposition against raising taxes for education, race also factored into the resentment. In many cases, opposition to raising taxes was largely led by white suburbanites, and those seeking additional resources were urban communities of color. The increasing presence of state government officials, particularly governors, in education policy emerged at a time when local communities of color were successful in their efforts to demand increasing state funding for local schools.

If the New Jersey experience is representative of a larger response to successful efforts by urban communities of color to secure additional state resources for local education, then we would expect to see state governments initiate efforts to pass laws that allow them to intervene in local schools in states where plaintiffs have been successful in the courts. Indeed, the empirical evidence supports this perspective. Every state takeover law passed between 1980 and 2000 came after successful school litigation efforts in that state's courts. Between 1980 and 2000, the incubation period for state takeovers of local school districts as a policy option, plaintiffs won school funding cases in 18 states (see Table 4.1). In 14 out of the 18 states where plaintiffs were successful, the states passed laws that allowed them to take over local school districts following the court decisions. Interestingly, the states that did not pass state takeover laws following court decisions were Montana, South Dakota, Vermont, and Wyoming. In these states, the average black population is less than 1 percent.

The evidence points to a connection between successful litigation efforts and the passage of state takeover laws. At the same time, the evidence also

Table 4.1. SCHOOL FUNDING PLAINTIFF VICTORIES, 1980–2000

State	Year of Plaintiff Victory in Court	Year of Takeover Law
Alabama	1993	1995
Alaska	1999	2003
Arizona	1994	2008
Arkansas	1983	2004
Connecticut	1996	1997
Kentucky	1989	1993
Massachusetts	1993	1991, 1993
Missouri	1993	2007
Montana	1989	No Takeover Law
New Jersey	1985, 1990	1989
New Mexico	1999	2002
North Dakota	1994	No Takeover Law
Ohio	1997	1998
Tennessee	1993	2004
Texas	1989	1995
Vermont	1997	No Takeover Law
West Virginia	1984	1992
Wyoming	1980	No Takeover Law

SOURCE: Education Law Center, "Education Justice. 'Equity' and 'Adequacy' Cases: Liability Rulings by State" (2017), http://staging.educationjustice.org/assets/files/pdf/Litigation/2017_Jan_Chart_of_P_and_D_Victor.pdf.

suggests that court decisions were not the only motivating factor. Race also seems to have played a role. In states where litigation was successful but a state takeover law was not passed, the black population is nearly nonexistent. The passage of state takeover laws following court decisions turned out to be problematic for communities of color. On one hand, the communities celebrated what they viewed as significant gains to address decades of inadequate schooling opportunities for students of color. On the other hand, the court victories were followed by state takeover laws

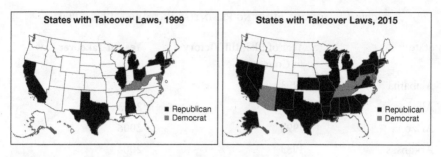

Figure 4.2. State Takeover Laws by State, 1999 and 2015

that thwarted their political momentum. Between 2000 and 2015, an additional 17 states passed state takeover laws (see Figure 4.2).

The passage of state takeovers laws had significant consequences for communities of color. In addition to affecting the ties between local political institutions and the schools, generations of students would be educated in systems that were under the direct supervision of state authorities. In Maryland, 60 percent of all black students in the state attend public schools in cities that are currently or have been under state supervision.[5] In Illinois and Pennsylvania, half of all black students attend schools in cities that are or have been under state supervision. In Arkansas roughly 40 percent and in Connecticut and Michigan roughly one-third of all black students attend public schools in cities that have been under state supervision. By comparison, in these six states, an average of 7 percent of white students attend public schools in cities that are or have been under state supervision (see Figure 4.3). These findings show that black students disproportionately attend schools supervised by state authorities, and therefore, are more likely to be educated in school systems governed by elected officials with political alignments and interests that conflict with the political interests of local communities.

SCHOOL DISTRICT ANALYSIS

So far, the evidence shows that laws allowing states to take over local school districts are mostly enacted by Republican governors. The evidence

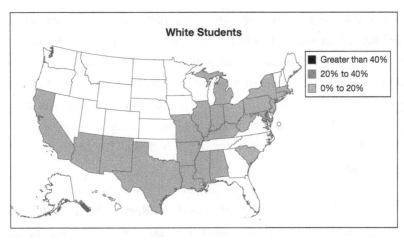

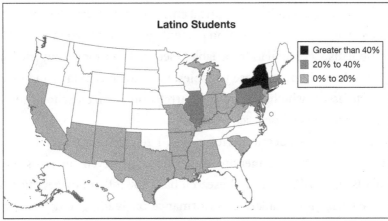

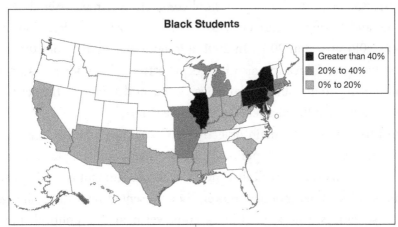

Figure 4.3. Percentage of States' Overall Student Population in Takeover Cities by Race/Ethnicity, 2010

also seems to suggest that there may be a relationship between communities' successful school funding litigation and the passage of state takeover laws. These two factors—partisanship and resources—seem to have had an effect on states' decisions to pass state takeover laws. To further explore the factors that may influence the decision to take over a local district I conduct a number of empirical tests using an original data set of nearly 1,000 U.S. school districts, which includes data for the years 1991 through 2006.[6]

In the first analysis, I examine the factors that are associated with a state takeover of a local school district. The dependent variable in the analysis is "Takeover" (0 = not taken over; 1 = taken over).[7] The independent variables include a number of political empowerment variables (black and Latino mayor and black and Latino percentage of the city council) and city and school district population variables (see Table 4.2 for a complete list of variables). In addition to those variables, I include local, state, and federal revenue to assess whether there is a correlation between school funding and state takeovers of local school districts.

To control for academic performance, I rely on a measure of family income since there is no measure of academic achievement across every school district in the data set. Research has shown that poverty levels are associated with low academic performance on reading and mathematics assessments as well as high school completion (Andrews et al. 2003; Lacour and Tissington 2011; Orfield and Eaton 1996; Owens, Reardon, and Jencks 2016; Reardon 2011). In 2001, a longitudinal study from the U.S. Department of Education also linked poverty levels to adverse student achievement. To measure level of poverty, the models include the percentage of students in the district eligible for free lunch.

In this analysis, the main objective is to examine whether there is a correlation between black political empowerment and state takeovers of local school districts. Recall that the theoretical argument is that as black communities gained political power, they presented political challenges to conservatives, who viewed black empowerment as a political threat. As the Newark case has demonstrated, and the empirical results thus far have shown, state takeovers have been led by Republican governors and

Table 4.2. DEPENDENT AND INDEPENDENT VARIABLES SUMMARY STATISTICS

Variable	Mean	SD	Minimum	Maximum
Dependent Variable				
Takeover	0.033	0.179	0	1
Independent Variables				
Black Mayor	0.096	0.297	0	1
% Black City Council	0.153	0.242	0	1
Latino Mayor	0.070	0.266	0	1
% Latino City Council	0.075	0.206	0	1
City Population	126,140	394,071	60	8,008,278
Black % of City Population	0.196	0.213	0	0.981
Latino % of City Population	0.208	0.236	0	0.986
White % of City Population	0.543	0.253	0	0.997
Total District Population	12,905	31,652	142	667,273
Black % of District Population	0.241	0.267	0	1
Latino % of District Population	0.278	0.302	0	0.994
White % of District Population	0.427	0.305	0	1
School District Local Revenue	$30,000,000	$93,000,000	0	$1,720,000,000
School District State Revenue	$38,700,000	$81,500,000	0	$1,690,000,000
School District Federal Revenue	$4,588,437	$17,400,000	0	$556,000,000
District % Free Lunch	0.481	0.176	0	0.996

seem to be motivated by resource-driven conflict. The next step is to learn whether black political empowerment has any role in the decision to take over school districts.

An analysis of the descriptive statistics show that black (10 percent) and Latino (7 percent) mayors account for roughly 17 percent of mayors in the sample. The mean percentage for black city council members in the sample is 15 percent, compared with 7 percent for Latino city council members. In terms of city populations in the sample, the mean population is 126,140. The mean for black and Latino percentages of the population is 20 percent for each, and the white mean is 54 percent. In terms of student population, the mean school district in the sample is 12,905. The mean for black students is 24 percent; for Latinos, 28 percent; and for whites, 43 percent.

The results from the analysis show support for the black political empowerment hypothesis. The results show that after controlling for poverty levels, an increase in the percentage of black city council members is associated with an increase in the likelihood of a state takeover as well (see Table 4.3). Cities that have less than 10 percent black membership on the city council have a less than 5 percent chance of having their school district taken over by the state. The chances of a state takeover double if a city has 50 percent black membership on the city council. The likelihood of a state takeover of a local school district increases to nearly 15 percent in cities where blacks represent over 80 percent of the city council (see Figure 4.4). Although the findings show that black city council membership is associated with state takeovers, the findings do not show that having a black mayor is associated with a state takeover of a local school district. Likewise, increases in the percentage of Latino city council members and Latino mayors are not associated with a state takeover at the conventional levels of statistical significance.

The findings also show support for the resource hypothesis: that is, increases in levels of state and federal resources for local schools are associated with the increased likelihood of a state takeover. Increases in state and federal revenues for local school districts are associated with a statistically significant increase in the likelihood of a state takeover.

Table 4.3. FACTORS THAT INFLUENCE STATE TAKEOVERS OF LOCAL SCHOOL DISTRICTS

Variable	Model 1	Model 2
Black City Council Members	1.72** (0.671)	2.20*** (0.750)
Black Mayor	−0.435 (0.375)	−0.747* (0.416)
Latino City Council Members	−0.418 (0.953)	−0.991 (1.18)
Latino Mayor	0.380 (0.572)	0.471 (0.703)
City Population	4.53 (6.09)	3.92 (6.32)
Black % of Population	1.35 (2.39)	1.35 (2.37)
Latino % of Population	4.19 (2.64)	4.15 (2.65)
White % of Population	3.15 (2.16)	3.06 (2.15)
Total School District Population	−0.0001**	−0.0001**
	(0.0001)	(0.0001)
Black % of District Population	−0.592 (2.22)	−0.824 (2.23)
Latino % of District Population	−3.51 (2.56)	−3.53 (2.55)
White % of District Population	−2.68 (2.22)	−2.79 (2.22)
School District Local Revenue	−7.04 (4.29)	−5.49 (5.17)
School District State Revenue	1.28** (5.90)	1.31 (9.21)
School District Federal Revenue	6.45* (3.22)	8.85** (4.42)
District % Free Lunch	3.26*** (0.855)	3.14*** (0.865)
Black City Council Members × State Revenue	—	−1.18 (1.03)
Black Mayor × State Revenue	—	6.91* (3.89)
Latino City Council Members × State Revenue	—	1.03 (1.43)
Latino Mayor × State Revenue	—	−6.06 (7.96)
Constant	5.70*** (2.14)	5.44** (2.15)
R^2	0.221	0.227
Observations	1,692	1,692

NOTE: Logit regression model (standard errors in parentheses).

$*p < .10, **p < .05, ***p < .01.$

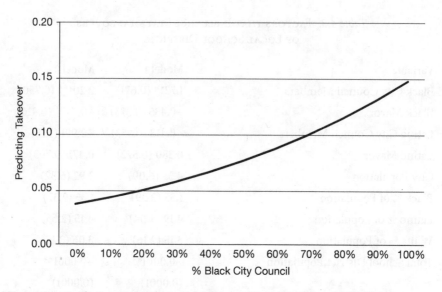

Figure 4.4. Predicting State Takeovers by Percent Black City Council Membership

In the second model, I included a number of interaction terms to assess whether the interaction between levels of political empowerment (representation on the city council and mayor) and levels of state revenue has any effect on the likelihood of a state takeover. The findings show that when interacted with state revenues, increases in the percentage of black city council members, increases in the percentage of Latino city council members, and Latino mayors are not associated with a state takeover. However, the findings do show a statistically significant association between increases in levels of state funding in cities with black mayors and the likelihood of a state takeover.

In the final model, I assessed the factors that affected the type of takeover that a state utilized when taking over a school district (see Table 4.4). Rather than treating state takeover as a dichotomous variable, I created a categorical variable to distinguish the different types of approaches states utilize when taking over a local school district. I use a multinomial logit regression to examine how the independent variables in our models may affect the type of takeover a district experiences.

The results from the multinomial logit regression show that compared with a baseline of no takeover, as the white population increases in a city

Table 4.4. Factors that Influence Type of State Takeover of Local School Districts

Variable	Elected Board Following Takeover	Appointed Board Following Takeover	No Board Following Takeover
Black City Council Members	1.03 (0.643)	2.19*** (0.778)	−0.212 (1.11)
Black Mayor	1.15*** (0.333)	−0.023 (0.414)	0.659 (0.587)
Latino City Council Members	0.480 (0.628)	−0.363 (1.41)	−148 (9865)
Latino Mayor	0.585 (0.378)	−1.34 (1.13)	−15.88 (4718)
Black % of Population	1.88 (1.90)	1.03 (3.92)	0.405 (5.31)
Latino % of Population	5.20*** (1.82)	0.558 (4.40)	−1.54 (7.00)
White % of Population	5.64*** (1.65)	0.954 (3.84)	0.661 (5.29)
Black % of District Population	−1.74 (1.60)	13.11*** (4.93)	3.43 (5.43)
Latino % of District Population	−3.51** (1.74)	12.69** (5.60)	1.75 (6.57)
White % of District Population	−2.90* (1.54)	7.88 (4.98)	0.606 (5.42)
School District Local Revenue	−1.50*** (4.81)	−1.07*** (3.91)	−8.28** (4.03)
School District State Revenue	−9.70** (4.78)	−5.99 (6.22)	3.67** (1.51)
School District Federal Revenue	1.58*** (4.82)	1.65*** (6.05)	−7.11** (2.87)
District % Free Lunch	4.00*** (0.658)	1.23 (1.09)	4.65*** (1.62)
Constant	6.53*** (1.52)	16.68*** (5.07)	7.41 (6.31)
R^2	0.332		
Observations	1,692		

NOTE: Multinomial logit regression model (standard errors in parentheses). Base outcome is district without a takeover.

*$p < .10$, **$p < .05$, ***$p < .01$.

that has experienced a state takeover, the district is more likely to experience the type of takeover where the elected school board remains in place.
Interestingly, the same applies to cities where the percentage of the Latino
population increases as well. This finding suggests that state takeovers may
not be having the optimal effect of increasing Latino representation on
school boards. As the previous chapter demonstrated, Latino increases in
population do not automatically lead to increased Latino descriptive representation on governing bodies. In some cities, Latinos have benefited
from appointed boards. As the Central Falls, Rhode Island, case has shown,
Latinos, who were previously excluded from political decision-making, were
aided by the school board appointment process following the state takeover.

The findings also show that compared with a baseline of no takeover,
black mayors are associated with an elected board following a takeover. On
the other hand, as the percentage of black city council members increases
in a city, there is an increased likelihood that the school board will be abolished following a takeover. Additionally, the findings show that as the percentage of black students increases in a school district, the likelihood of
the school board being abolished after a takeover increases as well. These
findings further demonstrate how takeovers have a detrimental effect on
predominantly black communities.

Although African American communities are more likely to experience
takeovers that result in the complete abolishment of the school board, the
results do not show that a black mayor and the black percentage on the
city council are associated with the no school board option at a statistically
significant level. However, that may be because the overwhelming majority of the takeovers that have resulted in the abolishment of the school
board with no replacement at all (90 percent) have happened after 2006
and therefore are not captured by this data set. As the analysis in chapter 3
showed, takeovers that result in the abolishment of a school board with no
replacement occur disproportionately in black communities.

In addition to the complete removal of the school board, black communities are also most likely to experience the closure of a school district following a takeover. Since 1989, seven school districts have been
taken over by the state and then closed or combined with a neighboring

Table 4.5. SCHOOL DISTRICT CLOSURES FOLLOWING A STATE
TAKEOVER: PERCENTAGE OF STUDENT POPULATION BY RACE/ETHNICITY

District	Black (%)	Latino (%)	White (%)
Altheimer School District, AR	63.5	1.0	34.0
Elaine School District, AR	71.6	1.4	27.1
Eudora School District, AR	22.0	9.0	65.0
Dollarway School District, AR	91.0	1.0	7.0
Richmond Unified School District, CA	14.4	47.7	8.7
Livingston School District, IL	95.0	0.7	3.0
Wilmer-Hutchins Independent School District, TX	78.0	19.0	2.0

school district. In five of those districts, black students represented the majority of the population (see Table 4.5). Again, black communities are more likely to encounter this school district experience compared with other groups. A burgeoning field of scholarship has begun to explore the effects of school closures on local communities, and much of the research has focused on districts that have experienced state takeovers.[8] In a study of community perceptions of school closures, Nuamah (2018, forthcoming) finds that blacks and Latinos, the groups that experience 90 percent of school closures, express low levels of support toward closures.

CONCLUSION

The empirical findings from this chapter show that race, economics, and politics are equally important factors that contribute to the likelihood of a state takeover, not just educational outcomes or concerns. The findings show that there is an association between increases in the black percentage of city council seats and the increased likelihood of a state takeover. The findings also show that there is a correlation between increases in funding from the state and federal governments and the increased likelihood of a state takeover. The results show an association between increases in state funding in cities with black mayors and the increased likelihood of a state takeover as well.

This chapter also revealed a broader argument about the role of politics and education. In chapter 6, I will discuss the implications of politics—particularly the *conservative education logic*, which has attempted to separate black political empowerment from the process of educating black children—in greater detail. First, we look at how the increasing presence of state governments in cities has altered urban governance.

The Implications of State Takeovers for Urban Politics

Cohesive and Disjointed State-Local Regimes

As previous chapters have shown, state takeovers of local governments are a relatively recent phenomenon in American politics that emerged because of the increasing presence of state governments in local affairs. Previous chapters have also shown that communities of color, particularly black communities with predominantly black political leadership, are more likely to experience a state takeover. Indeed, this book has argued that state takeovers emerged as a response to the rise of black political empowerment in U.S. cities. These two significant changes in American politics over the past 40 years—the increasing role of state government in local affairs and the emergence of black-led urban political regimes—lead to questions about how the intersections of these two factors have altered urban politics and the extent to which they challenge existing theories of urban politics.

In this chapter, I return to the Newark, New Jersey case to explore how the convergence of increasing state involvement in local affairs and the rise of a black-led urban political regime has altered urban governance. To examine these factors and their effects on urban politics, the theoretical focus will be on urban regime theory. Over the past 30 years, urban regime theory has been the dominant theoretical framework in urban politics.

However, urban regime theory has been criticized for its failure to incorporate the roles of race (Horan 2002; Kraus 2004; Nelson 2000) and state government (Burns 2002; Imbroscio 1998; Kantor, Savitch, and Haddock 1997) in its analysis of urban regimes.

. I will argue that the changing role of state actors in urban regimes requires an expansion of urban regime theory as a conceptual framework. The increasing presence of state actors, particularly governors, in local affairs has altered urban governance. As chapter 2 showed, in Newark, city officials were removed from the school district decision-making process following the takeover in 1995. After the takeover, the governor assumed a greater role in the city's governance decisions. Chapter 2 also showed that in Central Falls, Rhode Island, the emergence of a Latino electorate, which has become an increasingly important part of the statewide Democratic coalition in Rhode Island, has produced a mutually beneficial partnership between city leaders and Democratic state leaders. In Central Falls, Latino city leaders have been able to leverage their population's political participation to ensure that they have influence over local policies under the state-controlled regime.

The Newark and Central Falls cases suggest that as state officials, particularly governors, assume greater leadership roles in urban regimes, local constituencies have to contend with the presence of an influential regime actor whose electoral success may or may not be dependent on the communities that they lead. The implications of a greater state presence in urban localities has political and policy consequences beyond Newark and Central Falls and beyond school districts. As of 2017, Republicans control two-thirds of governorships and state legislatures in the United States. Republicans are less likely to rely on urban voters of color as an important part of their electoral or governance coalitions. As governors increase their roles in cities, the theoretical frameworks scholars utilize to analyze urban governance must account for these changes. Building on the argument that urban regimes should be viewed as intergovernmental regimes (Burns 2002), this chapter will argue that as states increase their presence in cities, local communities are best represented under *cohesive state-local regimes*, while localities are exposed to less desirable, even hostile, state-led policies under *disjointed state-local regimes.*

URBAN REGIME THEORY, STATE CENTRALIZATION, AND RACE POLITICS

Urban regime theory emerged as a response to the urban politics debates of the 1950s and 1960s, which were dominated by the pluralist versus elite perspectives of political power in cities (Bachrach and Baratz 1962; Banfield and Wilson 1963; Dahl 1961; Hunter 1953; Mills 1959). The pluralists argued that political power was diffused and distributed among groups, while scholars who subscribed to the elite perspective argued that political power was concentrated among the political and economic elite. For urban regime theorists, the elite and pluralist perspectives were limited, particularly concerning relationships among public officials, businesses, community groups, and other local political actors, which regime theorists considered the foundation of urban governance (Elkin 1987; Orr 1992; Stone 1989). Urban regimes, writes Clarence Stone, are "informal arrangements by which public bodies and private interests function together in order to be able to make and carry out governing decisions" (1989, 6). In sum, urban regime scholars argued for a view of political power that accounted for the power of the elites and the ability of the public to influence decisions at the local level.

In the urban regime, the "public" is represented by government leaders, who presumably are given the consent to govern and represent the citizenry through democratic processes. However, the growing presence of state actors in local affairs complicates our understanding of the public official in the urban regime. As governors assume a greater role in local governance, the "public," in the public-private partnership that is at the foundation of the regime, is still intact. Indeed, private interests may work well with state officials to carry out governing decisions at the local level. Moreover, the local citizenry may consider governors legitimate representatives of their interests on local matters. Therefore, the presence of state actors in local governance does not disqualify urban regime theory as a conceptual framework.

Conversely, there is also the possibility that governors and private interests may form alliances to make governing decisions that local citizens reject. Furthermore, local citizens may not consider the governor a legitimate representative of their local interests. In this scenario, the public-private partnership is still in effect; however, the "public" may not be representative of the local citizenry. Thus, while the increasing presence of state actors in local affairs does not disqualify urban regime theory as a conceptual framework, the presence of governors as leaders in urban regimes does require an expansion of urban regime theory in order to account for the degree to which the local citizenry is represented in the regime.

STATES IN THE URBAN REGIME

Scholars have challenged urban regime theory for its failure to account for how factors outside of city boundaries affect urban governance (Burns 2002; Imbroscio 1998; Kantor, Savitch, and Haddock 1997). Indeed, scholars of state politics have shown how state institutions establish the contours by which local officials exercise political authority. Frug and Barron (2008) point out that cities are not autonomous entities and that their powers are derived from state laws. Therefore, the arena in which local political actors can exercise power is structured and constrained by the laws that state legislatures have passed.

The institutional constraints on cities demand that local political actors create alliances outside of their urban spheres. Bridges (1984, 15) points out that cities are dependent on state and national governments and the permeability of their boundaries force local officials to work with political actors outside of the city to achieve their political objectives. Similarly, Burns et al. (2009) argue that state legislatures are central to the understanding of local policy outcomes and find that state legislature treatment of cities is influenced by the extent to which urban legislators are unified as a delegation. That is, when urban delegations are unified on an issue, they are able to ward off unwanted state involvement.

In his work on political machines, Steven Erie (1988) proposed an intergovernmental theory to explain why political machines were able to have a long-lasting, powerful presence in some cities and not others. Erie argues that powerful political machines emerged because of the intergovernmental alliances that local party leaders were able to forge with party leaders at the state and federal levels. Erie's work shows that relationships between party leaders at the local, state, and federal levels were critical in helping sustain local political machines.

Although the existing state scholarship has demonstrated that state politics is integral to an understanding of urban politics, these works do not account for the changing role of state government over the past four decades, when there has been a shift to greater state centralization and local governance transitioned from white-led political machines to black-led urban regimes. Furthermore, while the scholarship has emphasized the importance of state legislatures in understanding urban politics, we know less about the role of governors as local regime actors.

As chapter 4 demonstrated, gubernatorial power has grown since the 1960s. Indeed, scholars have shown how governors have exercised greater authority over a number of policy domains, including public education, over the past four decades (Barrilleaux and Berkman 2003; Bernick and Wiggins 1991; Lester and Lombard 1998).

To bridge the gap between the local focus of urban regime theory and the increasing presence of state actors in local affairs, Peter Burns (2002) argues that governors should be considered part of urban regimes and, therefore, urban regimes should be considered "intergovernmental regimes." In a study of Hartford, Burns finds that the governor in Connecticut has the authority to implement policy and allocate resources at the local level. Burns (2002, 68) concludes that leadership vacuums at the local level provide opportunities for governors to become bigger actors in local governing regimes.

This chapter builds on the Burns argument that urban regimes should increasingly be seen as intergovernmental regimes because of the increasing role of state governments, particularly governors, in local affairs. However, where Burns sees the growing presence of state actors in local affairs because of an absence of leadership at the local level, I argue that the growing state presence in urban affairs has been a result of political changes following the 1960s. As chapter 4 demonstrated, several factors, including race and political power, led conservatives to focus their attention on centralizing power at the state level. The centralization of power at the state level led to the increasing presence of state actors in city governance.

To examine how increasing state involvement in local affairs and the rise of black-led political regimes affect urban governance, I return to an examination of the state takeover of the Newark Public Schools. The Newark case provides the opportunity to conduct a comparative analysis within the single case study. Since New Jersey had Democratic and Republican governors in the period leading up to the takeover of the Newark schools, the state provides the ideal setting to examine political variation in state-local relationships leading up to the takeover. Moreover, since the Newark school district has been under state control for more than 20 years, and the state has had Democratic and Republican governors during this time, we can also examine the state-local relationship during a period of state control.[1]

NEWARK AND THE BLACK-LED REGIME

To summarize, recall that in the early 1970s, the transition to a black-led local political regime—a "black-led and black dominated administration backed by solid council majorities" (Reed 1999, 79)—had begun in Newark. In the 1970 municipal election, Newark elected three black city council members as well as the city's first black mayor, Kenneth Gibson (Rich 1996). In addition, during the 1970–1971 school year, nonwhites represented the majority on the school board for the first time in the city's history (Tuttle 2009). As blacks gained political power in Newark, their influence in New Jersey's state politics increased. In the state's largest city, in one of the most vote-rich counties in New Jersey, Newark's black political leadership gained influence beyond city limits, which local leaders utilized to bring resources to the city.

As chapter 2 discussed, black citizens and their political leaders in Newark and throughout the state of New Jersey challenged schooling disparities in the courts. The court victories in *Robinson v. Cahill* (1973) and then *Abbott v. Burke* (1985) were successful in bringing additional state resources for education to many impoverished communities, but they also introduced a new state monitoring regime in cities such as Newark that began to threaten black political leadership.

However, as long as the city's leadership could count on partnerships with state leaders, particularly the governor, local leaders attempted to leverage their power to influence the state's role in the city's affairs. In 1975, Democrat Governor Brendan Byrne, who began his professional and political career in Newark, as a lawyer and then deputy attorney general in charge of the Essex County Prosecutor's Office, ordered a state investigation into Newark's school finances, following a report from Newark's *Star-Ledger* about fiscal mismanagement in the district (Pratt 1992). The task force charged with investigating the district's finances recommended greater monitoring of the district, but Newark avoided more severe action from state authorities.

However, by the early 1980s, the political landscape began to change, and Newark and other urban districts began to experience greater oversight from state authorities. In 1981, Republican Thomas Kean was elected governor of New Jersey. Kean had promised to push for greater accountability from the urban districts. As chapter 4 showed, Kean and his Republican counterparts in the National Governors Association led a national effort to reform schools by asserting a more powerful presence of governors in the local schools. Under Kean's leadership, New Jersey's education commissioner, Saul Cooperman, implemented a more robust system of monitoring school district performance (Quinn 1988).

In 1985, the composition of the state's leadership also changed, and with it came significant consequences for Newark and other urban districts in the state. Along with a Kean landslide re-election, Republicans gained control of the state Assembly for the first time in 12 years (Stonecash 2002) and used their newly gained political power to demand greater accountability from the urban districts. In 1986, Kean proposed a law to the state legislature that would allow the state to take over underperforming school districts (Verdon 1988). The takeover law was passed by the state legislature in 1988. In 1989, the state became the first in the country to take over a school district when it took over the Jersey City Public Schools (Newman 1999). During the same time, state officials also notified Newark that its school district was being targeted for a takeover (McCoy 1988).

COHESIVE AND DISJOINTED STATE-LOCAL REGIMES

Governor James Florio (1990–1994)

As the state was moving toward a takeover of the Newark schools, the political landscape changed once again in New Jersey. In 1989, New Jersey elected Democrat Governor James Florio, largely as a result of votes Florio received from the state's urban centers. In the 1989 Democratic primary, Newark's Essex County, Jersey City's Hudson County, and Camden County accounted for nearly 40 percent of Florio's primary votes (see Table 5.1). Newark's Essex County not only played an important role in Florio's election but has represented an important electoral county for all Democratic gubernatorial candidates. Between 1965 and 2013, Essex County had the highest percentage of Democratic votes of any county in New Jersey (see Figure 5.1). As a Democratic stronghold, and the largest city in the state, Newark also represented a vital constituency to Democratic state officials, particularly governors.

Rather than move forward with plans to take over the Newark schools, Florio put a halt on the monitoring regime that the Kean administration had established. In 1991, Florio suspended all state monitoring of the school districts (Braun 1991). According to Florio's commissioner of education, John Ellis, the stoppage was meant to give the state time to come up with a more efficient monitoring system. Proponents of the state's

Table 5.1. JAMES FLORIO'S 1989 NEW JERSEY DEMOCRATIC PRIMARY
VOTE TOTALS BY COUNTY

County	Votes	Percent of Total Votes
Atlantic	5,772	2
Bergen	18,762	7
Burlington	14,997	6
Camden	30,777	12
Cape May	3,033	1
Cumberland	5,279	2
Essex	30,301	12
Gloucester	12,477	5
Hudson	34,273	14
Hunterdon	1,810	1
Mercer	10,744	4
Middlesex	16,499	7
Monmouth	11,890	5
Morris	7,587	3
Ocean	13,561	5
Passaic	8,594	3
Salem	2,511	1
Somerset	3,754	1
Sussex	2,257	1
Union	14,622	6
Warren	2,479	1

SOURCE: State of New Jersey Department of State, Division of Elections, "NJ Election Information and Results Archive," http://www.nj.gov/state/elections/election-information-archive.html.

system of monitoring school districts were unhappy with the decision. Leo Klagholz, who served on the state Board of Education at the time and would become the commissioner of education under a Republican administration, said, "Nothing in the law or administrative code allows the state to stop looking closely at the school districts to make sure they

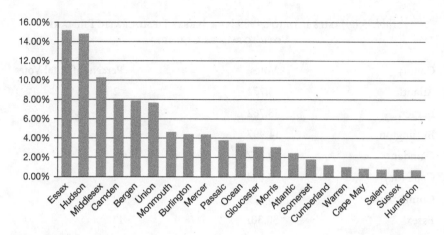

Figure 5.1. Average Percentage of Votes for Democratic Primary Gubernatorial Winner by County, 1965–2013

are abiding by the law" (Braun 1991). The suspension of state monitoring of school districts meant that for the time being Newark was no longer on the takeover clock.

In addition to not facing an immediate threat of a takeover, the city of Newark also received a significant increase in funding for its public schools during the Florio years. In 1992, Newark voters overwhelmingly passed a $523 million school budget, an increase of $100 million from the 1990 budget, a record for the state (DePalma 1990; Roberts et al. 1992). The state of New Jersey was responsible for nearly 75 percent of the total amount. The increase in funding was attributed to the *Abbott v. Burke* decision, which required the state to increase school funding for low-resourced communities, as well as the key role urban legislators and Governor Florio played in passing funding legislation.

During the Florio years, the Newark school district saw an increase in school funding and a decrease in monitoring. The political relationship between Governor Florio and Newark's political leaders was mutually beneficial and thus led to a period of decreased hostility between state officials and the city of Newark. During this period of a cohesive state-local regime, Newark officials were able to exercise influence over a state administration that relied on Newark voters for its electoral success.

Governor Christine Todd Whitman (1994–2001)

Although Newark's record school budget in 1992 symbolized a promise of opportunity for many in Newark, the state's wealthier districts mobilized to put a halt on tax increases and, therefore, a halt on school budget increases in Newark. In 1993, suburban voters succeeded in electing Republican Christine Todd Whitman as governor. The mutually beneficial political alignment that existed between Newark's political leadership and Trenton during the Florio years did not exist with Whitman's administration. The misalignment in interests was nowhere more visible than in the politics of education.

As chapter 2 demonstrated, Whitman promised "accountability" and to control public spending on education. Whitman's commitment to this promise was evident when she named Leo Klagholz, her first cabinet-level appointee, to head the state's Department of Education. Klagholz was an advocate of the state's monitoring of the schools and was a vocal critic of Florio's decision to suspend school monitoring. Soon after Klagholz was confirmed as commissioner, the state's efforts to monitor the Newark schools increased, and talk of a state takeover gained increasing attention.

In 1995, the state took over the Newark school district. The takeover had significant political and economic consequences for the city. Beyond the proposed academic reforms that the state would implement in Newark, the takeover undermined the city's political leadership and local economy. In addition to the removal of the superintendent of schools and the abolishing of the locally elected school board, the office of the mayor, which had always had a major presence in school politics, was replaced by the governor's office as the most influential political office overseeing the schools.

Governor Jim McGreevy (2002–2004)

Between 1995 and 2001, there was a *disjointed state-local regime* between Newark and the state administration. Politically, the governor and

Newark's political leaders were responsive to different constituencies. Despite the governor's influential role in Newark, Newark political leaders and the city's residents did not represent an important political constituency to the Republican governor. As a result, Newark's political standing vis-à-vis the state was negatively affected. However, in 2001, New Jersey elected Jim McGreevy, a Democrat, as governor. The McGreevy election was instrumental in forging a period of *cohesive state-local regime*, where Newark's internal politics were stabilized and the city—the community and its political leaders—experienced a different relationship with the political leadership in Trenton.

The 2001 McGreevy election solidified a new phase in the state-local relationship. In this new phase, there was an increase in community involvement in Newark's school politics. First, the state-appointed advisory board fully transitioned into an elected board by 2003. The 15-member advisory board, which had been appointed at the time of the takeover, transitioned into an elected nine-member board. Although it remained an advisory board, Newark voters were able to elect their representatives on the board. The elected board would eventually become a significant player in the political struggle for local control in Newark.

The second factor was that Sharpe James, who had been Newark's mayor since 1986, was a key ally of Governor McGreevy. From the early stages of the gubernatorial race, James had supported McGreevy. In fact, state Democratic leaders credit James for helping McGreevy secure the Democratic nomination, when other statewide political leaders were discouraging McGreevy from running for office (Haddon 2013). As a result, McGreevy's election meant that James and Newark were going to occupy a different status under his administration than they had during the Whitman years.

The third factor was McGreevy's appointment of William Librera as the state's commissioner of education. Librera did not believe that an extended state takeover of schools was productive and therefore began a process to attempt to transition governance of the Newark schools back to local control. Unlike Whitman's administration, McGreevy and Librera wanted to transition authority back to Newarkers. When the state had to decide whether to reappoint the superintendent, Marion Bolden, a native Newarker, or appoint a new superintendent, Librera left the choice to the community and the elected school board.

Following the 1995 takeover, the first state-appointed superintendent of the Newark schools, Beverly Hall, earned few admirers in Newark. By 1998, the superintendent was under mounting criticism from local leaders, particularly Mayor Sharpe James, who questioned the state's role in Newark. James cited reports that showed that Newark students were not performing any better after the state took over the district. Additionally, he complained that the state and Superintendent Hall had "funneled too many jobs and contracts to companies outside the city" (Alaya 1998).

In June 1999, Beverly Hall decided to leave Newark to take a position as superintendent of schools in Atlanta, Georgia.[2] When the search for the new superintendent began, Department of Education officials expressed an interest in having an internal, preferably local, candidate for the position. Just like in 1995, when state officials worked diligently to avoid looking like "colonizers" after the takeover, state officials were concerned with the perception of not having an internal candidate.

The state's internal candidate was Marion Bolden, the district's associate superintendent. According to Bolden, "The commissioner realized that if there wasn't an internal candidate, and we bring another outsider in, the community is going to be up in arms. So at least have a candidate, even though that candidate might not get the position."[3] Indeed, the state's intention was not to appoint Bolden superintendent of the Newark schools. However, when the top two candidates turned down their offers, state officials offered Bolden the job. The state offered her a one-year contract and less pay than was offered to the male candidates who had turned down the position before her. Bolden was offended by her treatment but decided that she was "going to prove them wrong, so I took the job."[4] On July 20, 1999, the state announced the hiring of Marion Bolden as Newark's new superintendent.

Marion Bolden was not only an internal candidate; she was also a native Newarker. Bolden attended the Newark Public Schools and after graduating from college, returned to Newark to teach. She had been a teacher and then administrator in Newark for 30 years before she became superintendent. Her appointment changed the tone in Newark. Whereas Beverly Hall was seen as an outsider unwilling to incorporate the wishes of the community into her decision-making, Bolden was seen as a local product who would surely seek to expand the role of the community in school governance. Teachers union president Joseph Del Grosso represented the sentiment of many in Newark when he said, "The teachers feel they have someone who understands the in-house problems and who is fair-minded and willing to listen" (Alaya 1999).

Local political leaders were also optimistic after Bolden's appointment. Sharpe James, who did little to hide his disdain for former superintendent Beverly Hall, was happy with Bolden's appointment. In his view, there was someone sitting in the superintendent's office who had Newark connections and would "play ball" with the local politicians. As it turned out, Bolden did not "play ball" the way James was hoping for, which led to a shaky relationship as the years went on. However, she did share the same philosophy with James about offering employment opportunities to Newark residents—to the extent that it was possible—stating that as superintendent, "I want people from the community in the schools because it is their children."[5]

Thus, the coincidental appointment of Marion Bolden as superintendent of the Newark schools represented a departure from the hostile politics that the state and the first state-appointed superintendent, Beverly Hall, had come to epitomize. When McGreevy was elected, many in Newark did not know whether Bolden would be reappointed as superintendent. Although she had many supporters, Bolden's relationship with Mayor Sharpe James had grown strained over time.

As rumors kept circulating that Bolden was about to be replaced because of tension with James, the voices in support for Bolden grew louder at the board meetings. At the November 2002 advisory board meeting a large crowd turned out to support Bolden. That evening, 44 individuals spoke at the meeting—the highest total since the 1996 mass firings. All but one spoke in support of Bolden. Students, parents, district employees, elected officials, community leaders, and clergy members defended Bolden's record as superintendent. The speakers pointed to improving test scores and Bolden's handling of the district's finances after Beverly Hall's administration left the district with a $70 million shortfall. Bolden's supporters came out in force at the January and February 2003 board meetings as well. However, despite the demands from the community to reappoint Bolden, the board, which had a pro-James majority, voted 5–4 to end her tenure as superintendent.

Librera, who attended board meetings during this period, considered the community complaints and decided that rather than follow the advice of the board, he would await the results of the upcoming advisory board election before determining Bolden's fate. According to Librera, if the election yielded results in favor of the candidates opposed to Bolden, then he would adhere to that wish. However, if the community demonstrated that they wanted to keep Bolden, by electing candidates who supported her, then he would listen to those voices. Librera's decision, which was supported by McGreevy, allowed local politics to decide who would be the next superintendent of the Newark schools. In the end, the April 2003 advisory board election was a resounding statement of support for Bolden. The pro-Bolden slate defeated the James slate by a two to one margin (Smothers 2003). After the new members were sworn in, the advisory board voted 7–1 in Bolden's favor. In an interview, Librera said the following about the process that led to Bolden's reappointment:

Although the decision was mine to make, I decided that so long as the board was conscientious, thorough, and responsible in the interview process, even though I was part of it, I said that I would support what they decide. Now that was purely something that I could do and I didn't need legislation. That is what happened in Marion's [Bolden] case. It was very clear to me that we made the right decision because leading up to it, there was gridlock. We left it up to the next election and see who would be elected to the board. They had three times the amount of votes they had before, so there was clear support for Marion. Marion had done a good job and was a credible candidate. This process fulfilled what I wanted, which was to get the community involved and have the community responsible for who the superintendent was.[6]

These factors contributed to a restoration of local politics in the Newark schools. In addition, the advisory board worked collaboratively with the state authorities. Although the board was "advisory," and the superintendent did not have to adhere to it wishes or demands, Bolden said, "I understood that the board represented the community and that the community voice had to be included in the district's governance."[7] Bolden and Librera's approach to the community created an environment where the board did not feel like the state had an imposing presence. Richard Cammarieri, who served on the board from 2002 to 2008, recalled his early years on the board as a time "when we had very little interference from the state."[8]

Additionally, Newark residents who attended the school board meetings were largely silent on the issue of state control in the early 2000s. Since the 1960s, the board meetings had become a place where Newarkers, particularly members of Newark's black community, would come to voice their grievances. Therefore, it was telling that the community members who attended the school board meetings voiced very few complaints about the state intervention in the early 2000s. Between 2002 and 2008, there were only 11 mentions of state or local control at the board meetings, compared with 29 mentions of state or local control between 1995 and 1998.[9]

The political climate in Newark stabilized during the cohesive state-local regime. In addition, there is also evidence that educational outcomes improved during this period. Between 2002 and 2008, the district's graduation rate increased from 49 percent to 72 percent (Association for Children of New Jersey 2008). During the same period, the gap between black male graduation rates in Newark and the national white male graduation rate nearly closed (Holzman 2010). Additionally, math scores on the state's High School Proficiency Assessment also improved (State of New Jersey Department of Education 2008).

THE END OF THE BLACK-LED REGIME IN NEWARK

Governor Jon Corzine (2006–2010) and the Emergence of Mayor Cory Booker

During the Democratic administration of Jim McGreevy, Newark's local elected officials and the state administration had a cohesive state-local regime. Despite the district's steady academic gains during this period, by 2007, there were signs that the period of cohesive state-local regime was starting to collapse. The business community, led by Prudential Financial in Newark but which also included Wall Street backers, was interested in advancing a school reform agenda that in their view required new leadership in the city for its success (Russakoff 2015). In their effort to unseat Mayor Sharpe James and replace the school leadership, business leaders supported Cory Booker, a city council member from the city's Central Ward, in the 2002 mayoral election, a race that Booker lost to James.

Although Booker was supported by the business community in and outside of Newark, the city's black community was ambivalent about the young African American Democrat, who grew up in Harrington Park, a wealthy suburb 20 miles north of Newark. In the 2002 election, Booker earned 47 percent of the vote, but his weakest performance came in Newark's predominately African American wards (Gillespie 2012). In 2006, Booker ran against longtime Newark city councilman and state senator Ron Rice for mayor, after Sharpe James decided not to seek a sixth term. Booker soundly defeated Rice, but as in the 2002 campaign, Booker's weakest performance was among the city's black voters (Gillespie 2012).

Unlike that of the two previous black mayors before him, who gained the mayoralty based on strong black support and were considered "unknown" variables among the city's business community, Booker's rise to political power in Newark was the opposite. He was supported by the city's business class and was a lesser-known figure in the city's black community. At the same time, Booker was the first mayor since the establishment of the public school system in Newark who was elected at a time when the mayor did not have direct influence over the city's schools.[10] Unlike those of other

big-city mayors and mayoral candidates, who place public education on
the top of their agenda, Booker's campaigns were largely silent on education (Gillespie 2012).

Although education policy was not a prominent campaign theme for
Booker, he had a vision for Newark's schools that consisted of reforms
that were considered controversial by many in Newark, including the
expansion of charter schools, school vouchers, and merit pay for teachers
(Mooney 2013; Russakoff 2015). However, since the state controlled the
Newark school district, Booker did not have to subject these reform policies to public scrutiny during his campaign for mayor. Yet, once elected,
Booker exercised influence over school policies despite not having formal
authority over the public schools.

In 2007, Mayor Booker began orchestrating the ouster of Superintendent
Marion Bolden, which led to her resignation in 2008 (Curvin 2014).
Booker wanted new leadership for the school district, and Jon Corzine,
who was elected governor in 2006 and had authority over the school district, supported Booker.[11] Thus, education policy in Newark, including
the ouster of the superintendent, seemed to be supported by a cohesive
state-local regime. The Democratic governor, the city's black mayor, and
the business community were working together to advance an education
agenda in Newark.

However, despite the appearance of the public sector working together
with the private sector, the public and its elected officials, including the
majority-black school board and city council, were increasingly excluded
from school governance decisions. At school board meetings, citizens
expressed dissatisfaction with Booker's growing influence over school
affairs without community input.[12] Eventually, the city council would also
join the school board and a frustrated community in voicing frustration
with the lack of community input on school matters, which included hiring
personnel, awarding contracts, and the use of public buildings.[13] Booker's
rise to Newark's mayoralty combined with the return of a Republican governor in 2009 represented the emergence of a disjointed state-local regime
that had significant political implications for Newark. Equally as concerning for the black community, the black-led regime, which was established

by black mobilization at the school level, was no longer part of decision-making at the schools.

Governor Chris Christie

In 2009, Chris Christie, a Republican, was elected governor of New Jersey. From the beginning of his administration, Christie made several decisions concerning the Newark schools that removed authority from local actors in Newark. During the press conference to announce the appointment of Cami Anderson, a Cory Booker ally, as his choice to run the Newark school district, Governor Christie was asked whether he would consider returning the Newark schools to local control, and he responded, "Absolutely not" (Calefati 2011). Christie's response to the question of local control angered many in Newark and set a tone that led to a hostile climate between the state government and the community.

Governor Christie and his superintendent of Newark schools, Cami Anderson, began implementing a set of reforms that were considered unpopular by many in the community, and this led to a dramatic increase in community engagement at school board meetings. Additionally, the teachers union, which has had a history of conflict and collaboration with the community (Golin 2002), saw the reforms as an effort to undermine it. Anderson's reforms included the expansion of charter schools, school closures, and teacher merit pay. The teachers union, parents, community leaders, and elected officials coalesced against the Christie and Anderson reforms.

In response, Newarkers demonstrated their concerns about the proposed reforms by increasing their presence at school board meetings. On average, more than 200 people attended the monthly board meetings during the 2012–2013 school year.[14] On several occasions, the meetings had well over 300 people in attendance. The number of speakers also increased. Between 2005 and 2009, an average of 10 people spoke at each monthly board meeting. Between 2010 and 2013, during the first Christie administration, the number of speakers doubled.[15] The increase in community participation was in response to the administration's unwillingness to take into account the voices of the community. Nearly 63 percent of all the comments referenced state control of the schools and the administration's efforts to implement school reform, including school closings, without input from the community.[16]

In addition to the strained relationship between the community and Superintendent Anderson, the relationship between the advisory board and the administration soured as well. Although it has been an "advisory board" since the takeover in 1995, during the Bolden years, the board functioned in many ways like a regular school board. The board worked collaboratively with the state on personnel and policy decisions. However, the Christie and Anderson administration not only stripped the board of these responsibilities but often did not seek its advice or input.

During the 2012–2013 school year, the advisory board chair was Antoinette Baskerville-Richardson. In addition to being a native Newarker, she taught in the Newark schools for more than 30 years. As the state administration increasingly insulated itself from the community, Baskerville-Richardson emerged as one of the leaders in Newark's effort to regain local control of the schools. Publicly, she questioned the state administration and its refusal to work with the elected board on any issue. In a conversation with Baskerville-Richardson, she stated:

> Past superintendents, even state-appointed superintendents, were savvy enough to still allow the board a lot of decision-making. It was not that they never vetoed anything, but it was far and in between . . . . For us, it has become a very unfortunate situation. Cami Anderson's inability to develop a working relationship with the board and the community and an inability to compromise is unfortunate. That is very important. Especially for the board because everything that we suggest gets knocked down. Everything we asked for gets denied. Even if it's things that for me would just make simple sense for an administrator to say, "OK, let them have that, I don't care." We don't even get those simply, minor things.[17]

As a result of the ongoing tension between Anderson and the board, the board went forward with an unprecedented set of measures. First, in March 2013, the board voted against Anderson's proposed budget (Elliott 2013). Then, in April 2013, the board unanimously voted "no confidence" in Superintendent Anderson (Calefati 2013). At that April board meeting, Baskerville-Richardson read the resolution, which stated, "Let it be resolved, the Newark Board of Education has no confidence in the vision, leadership, and direction of the state-appointed superintendent, Cami Anderson."[18] In addition to the no-confidence vote, the advisory board also approved a resolution to change its name from the Newark Public Schools Advisory Board to the "Newark Board of Education" as an act of defiance against the state administration.

Despite the growing tension and demands for greater input, Governor Christie remained steadfast in his plan to push through his agenda without the consent of the community. At a September 2013 press conference, when asked about growing community concerns with Anderson and the schools, Christie said, "I don't care about the community criticism" of Anderson: "We run the school district in Newark, not them" (Rundquist 2013).

As the disjointed state-local regime increasingly excluded the public from school governance, it created opportunities for nonpublic entities to influence school policies. In Newark, foundations have played a particularly influential role in education policy (Reckhow 2013; Russakoff 2015). In many instances, the role of foundations is shielded from public scrutiny. The most prominent example of a private foundation taking a role in Newark is the Foundation for Newark's Future, which was created with a $100 million donation from Facebook founder and CEO Mark Zuckerberg. The first time Newarkers heard about the donation and the partnership among Governor Christie, Mayor Booker, and Zuckerberg was on the *Oprah Winfrey Show* (Russakoff 2015).

Christie's rhetoric and the actions of state officials served to provoke further anger among Newarkers. In addition to demands for a greater say on school policy, the demand for local control increased at the advisory board meetings as well. A content analysis of Newark school board minutes from 1995 to 2013 shows that since the state takeover of the district in 1995, the issue of "state control" and "local control" has received the most attention during the periods of a disjointed state-local regime, when Republicans have held the governor's seat (see Figure 5.2). However, the mentions of state and local control have increased significantly during the Christie administration. During the Whitman years (1995–2001) there were 29 mentions of state or local control. Between 2001 and 2009, during the Democratic administrations of McGreevy, Cody, and Corzine, there were 12 mentions of state or local control. Under the Christie administration (2010–2013) there were 92 mentions of state or local control.

The lack of response from Christie and Anderson also prompted a response from the city council, although it does not have any authority over school governance. In May 2013, the city council voted unanimously to approve a resolution introduced by then–South Ward City Councilman Ras Baraka, calling for a "moratorium on all school initiatives" (Giambusso 2013). Newark voters also supported efforts to gain local control by

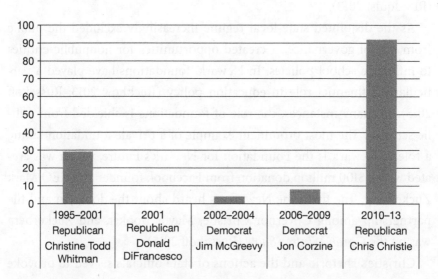

Figure 5.2. Number of "Local Control" Mentions at Newark Advisory Board Meetings since State Takeover in 1995

SOURCE: Newark Public Schools Advisory Board meeting minutes.

electing Baraka mayor of Newark in 2014. Baraka, a former high school principal, made the Newark Public Schools and the fight to regain local control a central focus of his campaign (Cody 2014). Despite the actions of the Newark voters, the elected school board, the city council, and the newly elected mayor, Newark residents and their elected officials still do not have authority over their school district. As it is a state-controlled school district, school governance authority rests with the governor. In the 2013 gubernatorial election, Republican Chris Christie was re-elected and won every county in the state except Newark's Essex County (State of New Jersey Department of State, Division of Elections 2013).

CONCLUSION

As the Newark case demonstrates, the growing presence of state government in local affairs has significant implications for our understanding of state politics, race politics, and urban governance. In Newark, as blacks gained political power in the city and were successful in increasing state resources for education, the city became increasingly vulnerable to intervention from state officials. However, a *cohesive state-local regime* decreased the likelihood that the state would take over the school district, despite state monitoring of the district since the 1970s. On the other hand, the election of a Republican governor, who did not depend on Newark voters or their elected officials for political success, led to a *disjointed state-local regime*, which increased the likelihood of a takeover in Newark. In 1995, after years of threats to take over the school district, the state's Republican administration moved to take over the Newark schools.

Over the next 20 years, Newark would experience the role of the state differently in the city, depending on which political party controlled the governorship. Although partisan identification was a major factor in helping produce cohesive or disjointed state-local regimes, the Newark case shows that co-partisanship does not have to equate to cohesive intergovernmental regimes. Cory Booker, a Democrat, played an influential role in the transition from a cohesive to a disjointed state-local regime in Newark, primarily because of the support he received from Newark's business community.

Booker's reliance on the business community allowed him to become the first African American mayor in Newark who did not receive strong support from the city's black community. Thus, Booker's support from the business community and his alliance with the Republican governor, Chris Christie, on education policy contributed to and strengthened a disjointed regime, which included the school board, city council, and Newark voters, on one hand, and the mayor, governor, and business community, on the other. In other words, Booker's mayoralty presented the appearance of a black-led urban regime; however, the majority-black city council and school board were not supportive of the agenda. More importantly, these participants in the black regime in Newark were removed from the decision-making process in the Newark schools.

Additionally, as the role of the public decreased during the disjointed state-local regime, foundations were able to increase their presence in the regime. Although the Zuckerberg donation brought attention to the role of philanthropic dollars in Newark, the presence of foundations is not unique to Newark. In her work on the role of foundations in the public schools, Reckhow (2013) finds that state takeovers of local school districts are likely to increase the presence of foundations in the district. The presence of foundations adds another layer of influence in the public schools that often operates away from public scrutiny.

The Newark experience illustrates how relationships between local regimes and state administrations can have an effect on state policy. The findings from this study suggest that collaboration, a key aspect of successful school improvement efforts, is most likely to occur under cohesive state-local regimes. However, in most cases involving takeovers in black communities, the encounter between state officials and the local community has been hostile. The separation of education policymaking from the community that has occurred in Newark and other cities that have experienced takeovers has significant political implications for communities of color.

Finally, the implications of disjointed state-local regimes have political and policy consequences beyond school districts. Early in 2016, a crisis emerged over lead contamination of the water supply in Flint, Michigan. The nation learned that the city was grappling with a poisoned water supply and that many residents, mostly children, faced the harsh reality of living with the effects of lead poisoning. Flint residents were told that several factors contributed to the city's poisoned water, including old, corrosive pipes. However, the major reason Flint residents had contaminated water in their homes had to do with a decision by government officials to switch the water supply from Lake Huron—the water source for many localities in the region—to the Flint River, as a cost-saving measure.

In most U.S. cities, local governments are responsible for decisions concerning the local water supply. However, local residents and their local elected officials in Flint do not have decision-making authority over their water supply. In Flint, the local government was placed in state receivership in 2011. The decision to switch the water supply as a cost-saving measure was made by an emergency manager appointed by Republican Governor Rick Snyder.

Snyder, whose electoral and governance coalitions are not dependent on Flint voters, who are mostly black and Democrats, ignored the complaints in Flint. For months, the community had raised concerns about their water. Flint residents did what democracy requires of a concerned citizenry by taking their concerns from their homes to their city hall. Despite their concerns and their demands for action, for months, state officials did not respond. The emergence of state takeovers and the increasing presence of governors in local affairs have significant implications for democracy in cities throughout the United States.

Takeovers and American Democracy

In June 1966, at a rally in the Mississippi Delta, a young civil rights leader named Stokley Carmichael shouted, "What we want is Black Power!" to an audience who, like Carmichael, had become increasingly frustrated with the civil rights movement's inability to eradicate black economic and political oppression. To Carmichael, the audience, and a growing segment of America's black population, at a minimum, "Black Power" demanded that blacks have access to the political institutions in the communities where they dwelled.

By the late 1960s, blacks had come to represent significant portions, and in some cases the majority, of the population in several U.S. cities. Despite their population sizes, however, blacks were prevented from gaining political power in many of these cities. As a result, a collision between frustrated black populations and a defiant white power structure led to uprisings in 163 U.S. cities in 1967 alone, including Detroit and Newark (Sugrue 2008, 325). That several American cities went up in flames as a result of a failure of political incorporation challenged the principles of the American pluralist system celebrated by scholars such as Robert Dahl (1961) and Banfield and Wilson (1963).

After the tumultuous late 1960s, the new decade ushered in an era when blacks began to gain political control of several U.S. cities. Although scholars pointed to the increasing number of black mayors, black members of the city council, and even black members of Congress to demonstrate the growth of black political empowerment, less attention was given to the role the public schools played in creating a path to black political empowerment. In cities such as Atlanta, Baltimore, Detroit, and Washington, D.C., blacks first gained seats on the local school boards before gaining seats on the city council and eventually the mayoralty (Henig et al. 2001).

The school board served as a training ground or "farm system" where would-be city council members and mayors gained political experience and exposure before launching campaigns for other levels of political office. Furthermore, the local school system had become the largest and most stable source of employment in many U.S. cities. Therefore, controlling the schools meant that blacks controlled a vital economic resource in their respective cities. Black community leaders, including the Black Power activists of the late 1960s, understood the importance of the public schools in the local political ecosystem.

Yet, roughly two decades after blacks began to gain political control in several cities where they constituted significant portions of the population, a new approach to reforming public schools began to emerge. The "takeover" of local school districts by state governments was added to the menu of policy options for states concerned with underperforming school districts.

Although the public schools fall under the purview of state governments, since the founding of the American public schools, local communities have been tasked with the responsibility of governing the schools (Tyack 1974). Therefore, the state takeover of local schools marked a shift in the relationship among the states, local authorities, and the community, as it relates to school governance.

As this book has shown, state takeovers of local school districts disproportionately affect communities of color. Cities whose school districts have been taken over include Baltimore, Boston, Chicago, Cleveland, Detroit, Hartford, Newark, New Orleans, New York City, Oakland, St. Louis, and Washington, D.C. When viewed through the lens of political empowerment, the list of cities whose school districts have been taken over draws attention. These are some of the same cities where the struggle for political empowerment was vigorously fought in the 1960s. Consequently, they have been cited by scholars as the cities representative of black politi-' cal empowerment (see Cruz 1998; Moore 2003; Orr 1999; Rich 1999; Rich 2006; Rivlin 1992; Sugrue 1996).

Therefore, only two decades after blacks began to gain political control of several cities, the state takeovers of local school districts seemed to threaten their political empowerment. Indeed, black community leaders in cities such as Baltimore, Compton, Detroit, Oakland, and Newark claimed that the takeovers were part of an effort to disempower the black community (Ansell, Reckhow, and Kelly 2009; Burns 2003; Orr 1999; Reid 2001). In addition to affecting African American communities, takeovers have also had an effect on growing Latino communities as well. Latino students represent 30 percent of the population in districts taken over by their respective states, and that figure will grow in the years to come.

Scholars have studied the effects of state takeovers of local school districts on educational outcomes. However, the aim of this book was to examine the historical roots of state takeovers and assess the political implications of state takeovers for the communities most affected by them—black and Latino communities. Indeed, the premise of the book is that we cannot understand state takeovers of local school districts without understanding the politics of state takeovers. Moreover, this book has also argued that state takeovers provide a unique perspective from which to view changing American race, state, and urban politics since the 1960s.

The book's initial empirical investigation explored how state takeovers affect descriptive representation on local school boards to learn how takeovers affect communities. Although this book is the first to systematically examine the effects of state takeovers of local school districts, the existing literature on centralized governance arrangements and their effects on communities of color suggests that state takeovers of local school districts would be detrimental to political empowerment (Chambers 2006; Fung 2004). However, I argued that the combination of centralization and race politics was complicated. Historically, racialized communities have had an ambiguous relationship with the state (national and subnational). The state both has sanctioned racial oppression and has been a powerful instrument in its demise. Therefore, relying on the state intervention literature, I hypothesized that state takeovers would disrupt existing governing regimes and that groups in power would be negatively affected by a takeover while politically marginalized groups would be provided opportunities for empowerment previously not available to them.

The results of the analysis indeed supported these hypotheses. For black communities, the racial group most empowered in the cities where takeovers occurred, descriptive representation on the school board was negatively affected by state takeovers between 1989 and 2013. Latinos, on the other hand, the group with the least political power at the time of the takeovers, appear to have benefited from a certain type of state takeover during the same period. In short, the findings suggest that the impact of centralization depends on the level of empowerment a community has at the time of the takeover. At the same time, the results of this study show how detrimental takeovers have been for communities of color, particularly black communities. The results show that majority–African American populations not only were more likely to be targeted for a takeover but experienced the most punitive forms of state takeovers.

POWERS AND LIMITS OF DESCRIPTIVE REPRESENTATION

By demonstrating that under certain conditions takeovers and centralization can actually lead to greater descriptive representation and political empowerment among marginalized populations, these findings buck conventional wisdom. Moreover, the results show how even symbolic representation can help spur broader political participation among marginalized populations. These findings contribute to an extensive body of literature that has examined the role of descriptive representation in our understanding of political empowerment.

Although the findings show that increases in descriptive representation had a positive effect on marginalized populations, there is a legitimate concern that appointed boards will lead to descriptive representation but not substantive representation of marginalized groups. State authorities are incentivized to appoint boards that are going to adhere to the state's plan for the district. In other words, the process of creating a state-appointed board may be a form of tokenism, and appointed board members may be silenced by state officials. Additionally, appointed board members may be chosen because their views align with the state regime and not the community that they have been appointed to represent. As Lester Spence (2015) has noted in his analysis of the "neoliberal turn" in black politics, local leaders, including politicians of color, may embrace policies that further erode the ties between communities and their local public institutions, such as the schools.

Despite these legitimate concerns, interviews with school board and community members and analysis of school board meeting minutes show that school board members challenged state authorities. As was discussed in chapter 2, in Central Falls, Rhode Island, an influential board member who was appointed by the state threatened to leave the board if the state did not address community-based concerns. As a result of this threat, the commissioner of education worked with this board member and other board members to address their concerns. The commissioner and the board members worked on a plan to remove board members who were not connected to the community and added new members who were supported by the growing Latino community.

In Newark, New Jersey, during the early years of the state takeover, several state-appointed African American board members challenged the state administration in public board meetings.[1] Indeed, several state-appointed board members challenged the state presence in Newark following the takeover.[2] Furthermore, these board members mobilized the community to attend school board meetings and challenge state authority in Newark.[3] Additionally, following the takeover, the newly appointed Latino members raised issues concerning the Latino community—such as bilingual education and contracts for Latino vendors—that were not raised at the board meetings prior to the takeover. Thus, although appointed board members are selected by the state and may follow the wishes of state officials at the expense of representing the concerns of the community, the evidence from Newark and Central Falls shows that such board members were attentive to the needs of the community and felt a responsibility to represent their communities. In some cases, the state worked in partnership with these board members, and in other cases, where the state was not responsive, these members became part of a larger movement to protest the presence of the state.

Although there are serious questions and concerns about the legitimacy of state-appointed boards following a takeover, the findings from this study support the argument that members of the black and Latino communities were advocates of their respective communities when they assumed positions on state-appointed school boards following a takeover. In cases where states appointed board members who were not connected to the community, the community—including appointed members of the board—mobilized to remove these individuals from the board.

Finally, there is an additional issue concerning descriptive representation that merits further discussion, and it is related to the broader issue of legitimacy to govern. In Newark, and other majority–African American cities, black political leaders had a limited opportunity to lead their cities. States began threatening to take over the schools only a decade after blacks had gained political power and eventually started taking over school districts two decades after blacks had assumed political control of their respective cities. In other words, black political leadership was challenged immediately after blacks assumed power in U.S. cities post-1960s.

The challenge to black political leadership was defended with two major justifications. The first was that black leaders were irresponsible government officials. In Newark and other cities that experienced state takeovers, state officials built a case to justify takeovers on the grounds that local leaders were engaged in corruption and patronage and "were incapable" of ending these practices. However, the history of urban politics is a history of patronage. From the late 1800s through the mid-1900s, machine politicians and nonmachine politicians in cities throughout the United States engaged in patronage. In Newark, city leaders, including mayors, had been charged with corruption years before blacks gained political power in the city (Krasovic 2016). Thus, the state challenge to black political leadership was based on a practice inherent to city politics, not black leadership. However, unlike previous groups, which had the opportunity to govern their cities for decades and fully participated in patronage practices, black communities and their political leaders were castigated for engaging in political practices as old as American politics. Although other ethnic groups previously had to endure challenges and questions about their ability or right to lead their cities, the emergence of black political power was unique in that it produced a response from state officials that gave rise to the takeover as a serious policy option. Previous groups did not experience state takeovers of their localities.

The second explanation states utilized to justify the takeover of local districts is potentially more problematic than the first. The act of a takeover suggests not only that blacks are not fit to lead their own communities but that they are not responsible stewards of their own children's education and well-being. For community members and activists, a major part of their struggle against state takeovers in black communities has been motivated by a resistance to this premise. In Newark, demands for local control have been denied by state authorities for more than 20 years. State officials have argued that taking over the school district and removing the district and community leadership from the decision-making process "is in the best interest of the kids." The idea that state officials, most of whom are white and not representative of the Newark community, believe that they are acting in the best interests of the children in Newark, and their parents and community leaders are not or cannot, is unacceptable to many. Marion Bolden, the former superintendent of the Newark Public Schools, said:

I participated in a meeting years after I retired as superintendent. The NAACP had a meeting with the commissioner of education, Christopher Cerf. When the NAACP went down and talked to Cerf, he said, "I'm going to do what's in the best interest of the kids. I don't care if that's not the democratic process." Can you imagine saying that to a bunch of black folks from the NAACP? He doesn't get it. And then he repeated something else about "I'm going to do what's in the best interest of the kids." I'm a Newarker, and I had to stop him. I said, "You are not going to be able to convince me or anybody else that you care more about my kids than I do."[4]

In Newark and other districts that have experienced a state takeover, questioning the merits of descriptive representation is part of a broader challenge that has deep roots in American history, meant to undermine the legitimacy of black leadership. Removing the local community from decision-making processes is problematic because it not only undermines black leadership but also attempts to send a message that these leaders do not know what is best for their own children. This view of racialized communities has significant implications for education, citizenship, and American democracy.

STATE TAKEOVERS AND THE CONSERVATIVE EDUCATION LOGIC

Conversations about the effects of state takeovers of local school districts have followed a similar trajectory to other conversations concerning school reform. Education debates in the United States often attempt to separate politics from concerns with academic achievement. Critics argue that despite increases in school aid, urban districts continue to fail to produce desirable educational outcomes. To address concerns with educational outcomes, reformers have turned to a number of strategies that have included increased accountability, testing, promoting voucher programs, increasing the number of charter schools, and taking over underperforming school districts. Although these efforts have expanded over the past three decades, broad sustainable reform has been elusive.

The arguments in this book attempt to introduce a different perspective to help explain why education reform has been difficult to achieve. By examining the politics of state takeovers of local school districts—their origins and their effects on local communities—we can better understand the influential role that politics, particularly state politics, play in shaping education. Educators and scholars have noted that historically, the process of educating children and young adults has been conducted with at least two goals in mind: passing on basic knowledge in the areas of reading, writing, and arithmetic *and* creating citizens. Although the reforms of the last 30 years have had a focus on the first goal of education, little attention has been provided to the second goal of creating citizens.

State authorities, educators, and even the scholarly community are all at fault—to varying degrees—for failing to focus on questions of citizenship when assessing the state of education in America. By examining the education process from a political perspective, which emphasizes the role of citizenship and the development of the citizen in society, an additional set of factors can be used to help explain the persistent and systemic failure of urban, predominantly black and Latino schools.

For people of color in the United States, the path to citizenship has been long and hard fought. At every step, the pursuit of citizenship has involved struggle and contestation. Following the Civil War, the period of Reconstruction advanced the citizenship rights of black Americans, only to be followed by a brutal period of Jim Crow laws. The era of Jim Crow was an effort to dismantle the notion of black citizenship.

By the mid-1900s, a civil rights movement gained momentum that helped to delegitimize Jim Crow laws and practices. In that effort, the public schools were an essential part of the movement. In addition to the *Brown v. Board* case of 1954, which ended legal segregation, communities in cities throughout the United States relied on school politics to demand their right to be recognized as full citizens. In the school arena, that meant that communities had the opportunity to decide who taught their children, what their children were taught, and how the resources of the school district were going to be allocated.

By the late 1960s and early 1970s, African Americans had made significant strides toward achieving full citizenship. The civil rights movement had helped produce legislation that codified equal citizenship. African Americans were also elected to political office at unprecedented levels. By the early 1970s, urban, predominantly black and Latino communities were also launching successful challenges to state school funding formulas, which were based on local property taxes and relegated their children to second-tier citizen status. The political gains meant that for the first time in our nation's history, black Americans, and other people of color, were beginning to engage in politics as full citizens. The public schools played a vital role in not only providing the venue for marginalized communities to assert their citizenship rights but also helping expose flaws in the democratic system that had produced and reproduced their political marginalization.

At the same time that blacks were gaining political strength and making significant gains toward full citizenship, a conservative movement at the state level was also gaining strength. Indeed, the argument in this book is that the conservative movement at the state level was buoyed by the emergence of black political empowerment in U.S. cities. The conservative movement, which by the 1960s had aligned itself with the Republican Party, was concerned with two major factors: (a) the rise of black political power, which had become a major part of the Democratic coalition, and (b) fiscal concerns emerging out of the successful efforts to increase school funding for low-resource districts. Increasing school funding meant that nonurban, wealthier districts would have to pay more taxes to ensure that poorer children, predominantly children of color, had an equal education.

The conservative response was to promote an education logic that professed to improve the education of urban students while undermining the political empowerment of their communities. The emergence of state takeovers of local school districts, which were led mostly by Republican governors and were adopted in states that had successful litigation efforts to increase school funding for low-resourced school districts, was only the most severe consequence of this education logic.

The issue with the *conservative education logic* is that despite professed efforts to improve education for communities of color, the interest has never been to produce citizens of color. By promoting black citizenship, and all of the rights and powers that accompany citizenship, conservatives would be forging a path to their own perceived self-eradication. The conservative movement in the states emerged as a response to black citizens' demands for power and the recognition of their citizenship. Thus, the conservative education logic has professed a concern with the education of black students and other students of color at the same time that it has invested in the political failure of their communities. However, as scholars have noted for centuries, the process of education cannot be separated from the process of creating citizens. Any attempt to separate the two at best produces a meager effort that inevitably results in failure.

The Newark example shows how the effort to separate the community and its elected representatives from the education process leads to hostility that stifles education. On the other hand, during periods when the community, its local leaders, education officials, and state officials worked collaboratively—*cohesive state-local regimes*—the Newark school district began to show signs of improvement. And yet, despite the evidence that education efforts work best when there is a collaborative effort, states continue to rely on a method of state intervention that seeks to eliminate local stakeholders from having an influence in policies that affect them.

In their efforts to promote the expansion of state takeovers of local school districts, proponents often point to the New Orleans, Louisiana, schools as an exemplar of the potential state takeovers have to improve educational outcomes in low-performing school districts. However, like other reform enthusiasts, supporters of the New Orleans takeover fail to account for the political realities and consequences of the New Orleans experiment. While proponents celebrate what they view as significant achievements in New Orleans, a brief examination of the New Orleans case points to how the state leaders in Louisiana epitomize the conservative education logic.

NEW ORLEANS, LOUISIANA

Following Hurricane Katrina in 2005, the state of Louisiana took over almost every school in the New Orleans school district (102 out of 117 schools). As a result of the takeover, the school district transitioned from a traditional public school system to an almost entirely charter school district. Almost overnight, New Orleans became the largest charter school experiment in the United States. Proponents of the New Orleans takeover have argued that it has led to improved educational outcomes in the city, particularly on test scores. Harris and Larsen (2016) find that math and reading test scores increased in the New Orleans schools post–Hurricane Katrina.

On the other hand, critics have argued that the academic gains are not as significant as proponents of the takeover claim them to be. Some have argued that the successes in New Orleans have come at the expense of the most vulnerable students in the district, who have been systematically "pushed out" of the district and not counted in the district's statistics (Gaboraug 2015). Others have argued that the effects of the reforms on educational outcomes are "mixed" (Gladwell 2015).

Thus, the district's gains have been subject to contestation. However, while researchers debate the claims concerning academic achievement in the district, the effects of the state takeover on the city's black political empowerment are not "mixed" or insignificant; the effects have been profound. Following Hurricane Katrina and the takeover of the schools, more than 7,000 city employees, mostly African Americans, lost their jobs (Carr 2014). Before the takeover, New Orleans had the highest percentage of black teachers in the country; roughly 75 percent of the teachers were black. Between 2005 and 2012, the number of black teachers in New Orleans decreased by 25 percent (Casey et al. 2015). As Sarah Carr notes in her book on the New Orleans schools:

> Over time, the state takeover and subsequent employee firing allowed for not only rapid growth in charter schools but the importation of a new group of teachers, principals, and education leaders. Control of the city's schools passed from a predominantly black political class to a largely affluent and white corporate elite. (2014, 66)

In New Orleans, the local school board, an important local political institution for historically marginalized populations, was stripped of its authority. In its place, a "recovery" board was created, which became the governing board of the New Orleans schools. After the takeover, many black residents viewed the traditional school board as nonfunctioning and powerless. Their withdrawal from school board politics led to a decrease in black representation on the school board. The takeover has depressed participation in school board elections among the black residents in New Orleans while providing an opportunity for whites to gain greater representation on the board. By 2008, whites represented the majority of the school board.

Additionally, the district became the first in the country where over 90 percent of the traditional public schools were converted to charter schools. By creating an essentially all-charter district, where governance authority has shifted to individual schools, the schools have shielded themselves from democratic pressures, mainly from locally elected officials and community groups. The implications for the city's black community, which, like in many other cities, has relied on organizing and collective mobilization to confront systemic barriers and challenges, including school-related challenges, are significant. As reformers and researchers tout the New Orleans reforms, the black community has not shared the same enthusiasm for the reforms. Surveys of New Orleans residents show that most black citizens in New Orleans do not feel that their schools have improved (Cowen Institute for Public Education Initiatives 2013).

In New Orleans, like Newark, Baltimore, Detroit, Oakland, and other major urban districts, the schools have had substantial challenges. However, the challenges have a long history, mainly rooted in the belief—a belief that was only systematically rejected in the 1950s and 1960s—that black children were not deserving of an education. By the 1970s and 1980s, the belief shifted from the undeserving black student to a focus on the undeserving stewards of the education of black children. The devastating effect that the state takeover has had on the New Orleans black community, which has included the loss of local employment, the removal of the local elected school board, and the removal of local city officials and the community from school decision-making, all justified on the merits of contested academic gains, is part of a perverse logic.

To be clear, this argument does not suggest that education challenges will be addressed by eliminating the conservative education logic. The

schooling challenges in our urban communities, predominantly communities of color, are a result of centuries of neglect, and addressing
these challenges requires comprehensive approaches. However, what it
does suggest is that what we know is required to improve education—
collaboration—can only be achieved when there is a recognition that the
success of black education is tied to the development of citizenship and a
community's political empowerment.

THE FEDERAL ROLE IN EDUCATION: RESTORING THE FEDERAL-URBAN AXIS

Given the conservative education logic, and the state takeovers of local
school districts that arise out of that logic, what can be done? For many,
the solution is found in deepening the foundations of local control. From
this perspective, strengthening the link between the community and its
local schools can create the opportunities to provide an education that has
the ability to incorporate the two main goals of education: passing down
basic knowledge and creating citizens. Although local control of schools
is desirable for many reasons, including the democratic principles it helps
foster, for marginalized, low-resourced communities, the concept of local
control is complicated. On one hand, local communities should be able
to determine who teaches their children, who works in their communities, and what is being taught in their schools, among other things. Local
control allows citizens to utilize the mechanisms of democracy to address
local concerns.

At the same time, low-resource communities have the challenge of
depending on resources from outside of their communities. The process of ensuring equitable education opportunities for students from low-
resource communities has involved demands for additional resources
from the federal government and state governments. Therefore, the challenge for advocates of local control is being able to attain resources from
federal and state sources without undermining the community's political
empowerment and the ability to determine the best path for the citizens

of the community. As the chapters in this book have shown, the goal of growing political empowerment while securing resources from outside of local government is problematic for communities of color. State governments, particularly Republican administrations and nonurban state legislators, including Democratic nonurban state legislators, are not interested in the political development of historically marginalized communities, particularly communities of color.

The lack of concern for and investment in the political development of marginalized communities presents the most significant obstacle to the educational achievement of students of color. As has been discussed, the process of educating students of color is inseparable from the political struggle of communities of color. Communities of color have gained access to education and the resources to educate their children through political struggle.

So, how can marginalized, low-resourced communities address this political/educational dilemma? Based on the findings in this study, one possibility is to minimize the power of state governments in local education. State governments have obstructed the political empowerment of communities of color. Furthermore, a dependence on political and partisan alignments between local government leaders and state administrations in order to create the collaborative climate that is necessary for improved education outcomes will not produce an institutionalized path toward sustainable achievement. Therefore, perhaps the solution may be found in revisiting the federal-urban axis that began to emerge in the 1960s, before state governments began to centralize authority and increase their presence in local affairs at unprecedented levels.

Removing state authorities from public education is not feasible or desirable. The U.S. Constitution places the responsibility of education on the states, and states have an important role to play in securing the education of their residents. However, there is ample space for the federal government to increase its presence in local public education. Since the 1950s, the federal government has expressed greater concerns about public education and increased its role in the public schools. However, several factors including concerns with "license and capacity" have limited the federal role in public education (Manna 2006). Most notably, federal resources account for only roughly 10 percent of local school funding.

Thus, while asserting greater levels of local control is an important and necessary aspect of democratizing the process of education, local democracy can be promoted by increasing the role of the federal government in the public schools. Local control can be bolstered by a more robust federal presence in public education in three key areas: (1) funding, (2) establishing stronger links between the federal government and cities, and (3) providing equal rights protections to communities of color that are politically marginalized by the actions of state governments.

The national government has the tools to increase its involvement by increasing funding. For marginalized, low-resourced communities, the level of federal support for education should be considerably higher than the roughly 10 percent districts have received over the past three decades. Federal resources for low-resource communities should increase to roughly a third of the revenue required to provide an equitable education. The remaining two-thirds should be divided between state and local governments.

In addition to the federal government providing additional financial support for low-resourced school districts, the federal role should include an increased presence in providing civil and political protections for marginalized communities. The state takeovers of local school districts in Newark and New Orleans, and other localities, in addition to the municipal takeover in Flint, Michigan, demonstrate that state officials can violate the constitutional right of political representation, without concern for reprimand. Thus, the presence of the federal government should be concerned with not only education but the political empowerment of communities. This includes local representation (mayor, school board, community groups).

The responsibility of ensuring these protections, similar to voting and civil rights, falls on the federal government. Therefore, the process of educating children must also include a guarantee of the political rights of an education, which consist of equal protection and the right to representation. State governments have not proven to have the interest or capacity to provide these protections. On these grounds, there is a constitutional justification to increase the involvement of the federal government in public education.

Although the Supreme Court has ruled that the Fourteenth Amendment does not guarantee a right to public education, the Constitution does provide protections for the political rights of citizens. The process of adequately educating individuals is inseparable from the political rights of those individuals and their community, and education should be viewed as a political right that the federal government should be compelled to protect when state governments fail to do so.

TAKEOVERS AND DEMOCRACY

In the United States, we have a representative democracy, where citizens elect the individuals who will represent them in governmental bodies ranging from the local school board all the way to the White House. A basic assumption in our democratic system is that elected officials must be, to some degree, responsive to the citizens they represent or else face the prospect of losing their seat. In other words, the threat of losing an election serves as a mechanism to ensure some level of accountability on the part of elected officials.

However, what happens when elected officials are not accountable to the citizens they represent? In Newark and Flint, and other predominately African American cities, states have taken over local government functions. As the findings in this book have shown, when states assume governance responsibility following a takeover, the extent to which local residents can still influence the policies that ultimately affect them is largely dependent on the relationship between the city and its state officials.

In Michigan and in most places where a state takeover of a municipality or a school district has occurred, Republican governors and Republican-majority state legislatures have been in power when states have taken over local governments. Most localities that experience a takeover have African American and Latino majorities and mostly identify as Democrats. Once they have taken over a locality, Republican administrations have implemented policies that local populations have often rejected because they disagree with the policies or because they were not able to have a voice in shaping policy. Despite the objection of local citizens, these state administrations have advanced their policies without fear of being held accountable, since these Republican administrations do not count on urban voters of color as integral parts of their winning coalitions.

The tragedy in Flint and disregard of citizenship in Newark demonstrate the dangers of state takeovers of local governments. Furthermore, the takeovers in these respective communities reveal a flaw in the structure of our American democracy that is only familiar to poor communities of color, particularly black communities. All Americans should be concerned with a structure that allows a segment of its citizenry to lose their right to have a say in the water their children will drink and how their children will be educated, among other things, with impunity.

As the results of this study have shown, a political environment where stakeholders are involved in the decision-making process is an important ingredient in providing the political stability school districts and local governments require to implement effective initiatives that can be successful in the long term. At the same time, local communities should also develop their own public spheres where groups can come together to sort out their politics. As blacks and Latinos increasingly find themselves sharing the same communities and political spaces, their local communities must carve out a space where they can discuss and address community issues separate from the zero-sum arrangements that accompany electoral politics. By establishing an inclusive public sphere, local communities can collectively decide whether to invite or challenge state intervention. The long-term solutions to their community needs demand their collaborative efforts. As this research has shown, in cities like Newark both black political empowerment and Latino political empowerment have been undermined by the absence of black *and* Latino political empowerment. As has been the case for historically marginalized populations in the United States, the establishment of an inclusive and collaborative public sphere begins in the public schools.

Epilogue

On January 18, 2014, Newark was once again at the center of the black political power universe, as it had been in July 1967, when the city hosted the first National Conference on Black Power. This time, generations of activists gathered in Newark to commemorate the life of Amiri Baraka (formerly LeRoi Jones), a poet, an activist, and one of the most influential black political and intellectual figures in the late 20th century. The ceremony was officiated by the actor and activist Danny Glover and included performances and poetry readings, including a poem written by Maya Angelou and read by Sonia Sanchez. The scholar Cornel West also spoke at the funeral, and the Rev. Jesse Jackson spoke to an audience of thousands the night before at Baraka's wake.

As speakers noted at the wake and the funeral, Baraka's death was also a moment to reflect on the struggle for black political empowerment in the United States—a struggle that Baraka and the city of Newark helped define in the 1960s and the decades that followed. That evening, Amiri Baraka's son, Ras Baraka, also delivered remarks and was welcomed by an audience that viewed the younger Baraka as not only his father's offspring but also the community's offspring. The younger Baraka, who was at the time a city councilman and the principal at Central High School in Newark, was a candidate for mayor and was viewed by many in the black community as a voice of the community. In May 2014, Ras Baraka was elected mayor of Newark.

Much like that of previous generations of black leaders in Newark, and in other cities, Ras Baraka's emergence as a political leader and mayor was shaped and propelled by school politics. In his campaign for mayor, Baraka made the fight for local control of the school district, which at the time had been under state control for 19 years, a central part of his campaign. In an interview, I asked Baraka why, unlike the previous mayor, Cory Booker, he had made the idea of local control of the schools a central part of his campaign, and he replied:

> It was both pragmatic, in the sense that we were being governed and the school system was not functioning the way we need it to function and still isn't 100 percent. In order for us to take responsibility of it, we have to control it. So we are blamed for problems that we have no control over. It seems to me that we should be able to control it. And symbolically, the issue of self-determination is important for me, particularly in us trying to move our city into a place where people begin to become accountable and responsible to each other for the way the city looks, the way it's moving, and what's going on. We have to take the posture that the city belongs to us and be prepared to run it and govern it in a way that we see fit. And local control is really symbolically part of a larger statement that the city belongs to us and we ought to be running it the way that we see fit and we ought to be in control of the engines that make the city go.[1]

Yet, despite the community's election of Baraka, and his promise to fight for local control of the schools, the authority to return the schools to local control rested with the governor. Since his election as governor in 2009, Chris Christie had rejected any notions of Newark gaining local control of its schools, which did not seem promising to Baraka and the city of Newark. However, in 2015, several events conspired to create the most significant movement in the effort to regain local control in Newark since the takeover in 1995.

In February 2015, a group of Newark students staged a four-day protest in the district's central office. Their aim was to demand an end to the unpopular reforms initiated by the district superintendent, Cami Anderson. The student "occupation" of the central office gained statewide and national attention. Then in May 2015, thousands of Newark students walked out of school to protest the district's school reforms. The students shut down a major intersection in Newark near several major highways. Again, the student protests gained statewide and national attention.

As the student protests gained momentum, there was another major political story developing in Trenton. Chris Christie was preparing to announce his candidacy for the Republican nomination for president of the United States. For Christie, whose candidacy would rely on a strategy of convincing voters that he was a Republican who had demonstrated the ability to win in a blue state, the student protests in Newark presented a challenge and unwanted distraction. Despite years of rejecting calls for local control and demands to remove the state-appointed district super-intendent, Cami Anderson, Christie changed course as a result of the student protests. Christie's response was to initiate a process that would lead to the ouster of the unpopular superintendent. Although the removal of the superintendent was celebrated by many, for Mayor Baraka, and other community activists, Anderson's removal was only one part of the objective. The main goal was to regain local control of the schools.

The demand that the issue of local control be added to the conversation led to the beginning of negotiations that would eventually produce a path to local control in Newark. On June 26, 2015, Christie and Baraka announced the formation of the Newark Educational Success Board. The board was charged "with developing a clear, specific pathway with appropriate timelines and benchmarks for the return of local control to the Newark community" (Pizarro 2015). Four days later, on June 30, 2015, Chris Christie officially announced his campaign for president of the United States.

As of summer 2017, Newark was preparing for what seems will be the return of local control after over two decades of state control of the school district. If it is achieved, it will be because of the political struggle of the community, which has involved the activism of students and community organizations, the role of the mayor, and the public resistance at school board meetings by parents and board members. Yet, as the city prepares for what seems to be the likelihood of local control, local leaders, particularly the mayor, are fully aware that the return of local control will be under serious scrutiny and in the shadow of the state.

If Newark is able to prevent another takeover, the mayor and other community leaders understand that all of the different sections and groups in the city have to work collaboratively, particularly African Americans and Latinos, the two largest groups in Newark. To help forge a collective ethos, in 2017, Baraka held a series of meetings throughout the city to discuss the process of gaining local control. In his remarks, the mayor asked citizens to "imagine" the types of schools that they want for their communities so that they can begin the process of transitioning from a posture of fighting for control to actual control. In this effort, Baraka has used the metaphor of a football game to convey the importance of shifting strategies, stating, "For too long, we have been on defense. And for many of us, that is all we know. Now we have to get used to playing offense and having the ball in our hands. We have to learn how to do that."[2]

Thus, as the city of Newark prepares to start a new school year in fall 2017, the city enters a new phase, with a new approach to an old effort of doing the best that they can for their children. If Baraka's metaphor is fitting, the challenge for this generation of Newarkers, as it has been for generations before them, will be how the city withstands the weight of the state's response—indeed, America's response—when they advance the ball.

State Takeovers of Local School Districts and Mayoral Control

Beginning in the early 1990s, several U.S. cities began to shift from locally elected school boards to a mayoral-led school governing structure (Wong and Shen 2003). In mayoral-led districts, the mayor appoints the school board and is responsible for the governance of the city's public schools. Interestingly, the majority of all mayoral-led districts were first taken over by the state before they became mayoral-led districts. In Boston, Chicago, and New York City, the state takeover was specifically designed to provide governance authority to the mayor. As of 2013, there were 17 mayoral-led school districts in the United States. Eleven of these mayoral-led districts were first taken over by the state before the district transitioned into some form of mayoral-led governance structure (see Table A.1). The cities of Baltimore, Boston, Chicago, Cleveland, Detroit, the District of Columbia, Harrisburg, Hartford, New York, Oakland, and Philadelphia were first taken over before they became mayoral-led districts.

Table A.1 List of Mayoral-Controlled School
Districts First Taken Over by the State

City	State Takeover
Boston, MA	Yes (1992)
Chicago, IL	Yes (1995)
Baltimore, MD	Yes (1997)
Cleveland, OH	Yes (1998)
Detroit, MI	Yes (1999)
Oakland, CA	Yes (2000)
Harrisburg, PA	Yes (2000)
Washington, DC	Yes (2007)
Philadelphia, PA	Yes (2001)
Indianapolis, IN	No
New York, NY	Yes (2002)
Hartford, CT	Yes (2005)
Los Angeles, CA	No
New Haven, CT	No
Providence, RI	No
Trenton, NJ	No
Yonkers, NY	No

SOURCE: List of mayoral control cities adapted from K. Wong and F. Shen, "Mayoral
Governance and Student Achievement: How Mayor-Led Districts Are Improving
School and Student Performance" (Washington, DC: Center for American
Progress, 2013).

State Takeovers by State, School District,
and Year of Takeover (1989–2013)

State	School District	`Year of Takeover
Alabama	Barbour County School District	1996
	Macon County School District	1996
	Wilcox County School District	1996
	Barbour County School District	1999
	Jefferson County School District	2000
	Birmingham School District	2012
Arizona	Colorado City Unified District	2005
	Peach Springs Unified District #8	2007
	Saddle Mountain Unified District #90	2007
	Union Elementary School District	2007
Arkansas	Altheimer School District	2002
	Elaine School District	2002
	Helena-West Helena School District	2005
	Eudora School District	2006
	Midland School District	2006
	Bald Knob School District No. 1	2007
	Decatur School District	2008
	Greenland School District #95	2008
	Helena-West Helena School District	2011
	Pulaski County Special School District	2011
	Dollarway School District	2012

State	School District	Year of Takeover
California	Richmond Unified School District	1991
	Coachella Unified School District	1992
	Compton Unified School District	1993
	Emery Unified School District	2001
	Oakland Unified School District	2003
	West Fresno Elementary School District	2003
	Vallejo City Unified	2004
	King City Joint Union High School District	2009
	Alisal School District	2010
	Inglewood School District	2012
Connecticut	Bridgeport	1988
	West Haven	1991
	Hartford	1997
	Waterbury	2001
	Bridgeport	2011
	Windham School District	2012
District of Columbia		1995
Illinois	East St. Louis School District	1994
	Chicago School District	1995
	Hazel Crest School District 152-5	2002
	Livingston School District 4	2002
	Round Lake Area Schools District 116	2002
	Cairo Unit School District 1	2003
	Venice Community Unit School District #3	2003
	Proviso Township High School District 209	2009
	East St. Louis School District	2011
	North Chicago School District 187	2012

State	School District	Year of Takeover
Kentucky	Pike County School District	1988
	Floyd County School District	1989
	Whitley County School District	1989
	Harlan County School District	1992
	Letcher County School District	1994
	Floyd County School District	1997
Louisiana	New Orleans School District	2003
Maryland	Baltimore City School District	1997
	Prince George's County School Dist	2002
Massachusetts	Chelsea Public Schools	1989
	Boston Public Schools	1991
	Lawrence Public Schools	1998
	Lawrence Public Schools	2011
Michigan	Detroit Public Schools	1999
Mississippi	North Panola School District	1996
	Oktibbeha County School District	1996
	Tunica County School District	1997
	Sunflower County School District	1999
	North Bolivar School District	2005
	Hazlehurst School District	2008
	North Panola School District	2008
	Indianola School District	2009
	Tate County School District	2009
	Okolona School District	2010
	Drew School District	2011
	Aberdeen School District	2012

State	School District	Year of Takeover
Missouri	St. Louis School District	2008
New Jersey	Jersey City Public Schools	1989
	Paterson Public Schools	1991
	Newark Public Schools	1995
	Camden Public Schools	2002
New Mexico	Santa Fe Independent School District	1999
New York	Roosevelt Union School District	1995
	New York City Public Schools	2002
Ohio	Cleveland Public Schools	2003
	Youngstown City Schools	1996
	East Cleveland Public Schools	1995
Pennsylvania	Chester-Upland School District	1994
	Harrisburg	2000
	Philadelphia Public Schools	2001
Rhode Island	Central Falls School District	1991
South Carolina	Allendale County School District	1999
Texas	Somerset Independent School District	1995
	Wilmer-Hutchins Independent School District	1996
West Virginia	Logan County Schools	1992
	Mingo County School District	1998
	Lincoln County School District	2000
	McDowell County Schools	2001
	Hampshire County School District	2006
	Fayette County School District	2010
	Gilmer County School District	2011

Newark, New Jersey, was selected as the primary case study for several reasons. First, New Jersey was the first state in the country to pass a state takeover law. New Jersey's efforts to pass a state takeover law were motivated by concerns with the Newark school district and other urban districts in the state, including Jersey City and Paterson. Second, Newark's district size and racial and ethnic demographics are similar to those of other districts that have been taken over by their respective states. Third, the Newark case provides the opportunity to examine how time and changes in levels of political empowerment may affect how communities experience state takeovers. Although the Newark takeover occurred in 1995, the state of New Jersey had initially proposed to take over the Newark schools in the late 1960s. Finally, as in most districts that experience a takeover, the state abolished the existing school board in Newark and replaced it with an appointed board. Therefore, the Newark case study provides insight into how other cities may experience a takeover of their local school district.

The Central Falls, Rhode Island, case was selected because it offered an opportunity to examine a city with a different experience with a state takeover. Unlike in Newark, the majority of the population in Central Falls is Latino. Also, at the time of the takeover, the city did not have any Latino public officials. Central Falls is one of the few cities that have experienced a state takeover under these circumstances. Lawrence, Massachusetts, had a similar experience with a state takeover. As the Latino population increases in cities throughout the United States, the Central Falls case is helpful in understanding state-local education and political dynamics.

For the New Jersey and Rhode Island case studies, several data sources were employed. Between 2010 and 2017, I conducted more than 70 interviews of state officials, district administrators, teachers, parents, and local leaders in New Jersey and Rhode Island. In New Jersey, I interviewed 44 individuals. In Rhode Island, I interviewed 28 individuals. The individuals were identified because of their public roles in school-related issues at the state or local level. I also interviewed public officials, parents, and teachers in Paterson and Union City, New Jersey, to learn about their experiences with the state takeover (Paterson) and the threat of a state takeover (Union City) of their local school districts. During the 2012–2013 school year, I attended every school board meeting in Newark, Paterson, and Union City.

For demographic data in each city and state, I rely primarily on the U.S. Census. I use several newspaper sources, most notably the *New York Times, Providence Journal,* and *Star-Ledger,* for historical and contemporary data. I rely on documents from the Essex County Clerk's Office, New Jersey Department of Education, New Jersey Department of State, and Newark Public Schools for voting records, teaching and staff data, and school board meeting minutes to conduct content analysis.

The Newark Public Library was an especially valuable source of information for this project.

Notes on Quantitative Data and Analysis

To create a sample of school districts I used several criteria. The data set includes states that have passed state takeover laws. The selected school districts have a student population of 3,000 or greater. The school districts are traditional public school districts (charter school districts are not part of the data set). Finally, the selected school districts have a student population with at least 50 percent free or reduced lunch.

Data used in chapter 4 were compiled from several sources. For African American city council and mayoral representation, I relied on the National Roster of Black Elected Officials by the Joint Center for Political and Economic Studies. For Latino city council and mayoral representation, I relied on the Directory of Latino Elected Officials provided by the National Association of Latino Elected and Appointed Officials. For descriptive representation data not accessible through the National Roster of Black Elected Officials or the Directory of Latino Elected Officials, I used a combination of strategies, including city government websites, newspaper sources, city council meeting minutes, and interviews with city officials.

For population data, I relied on the U.S. Census. The data gathered included total city population, percent black, percent Hispanic/Latino, and percent non-Hispanic white. For school district data, I relied on the U.S. Department of Education's National Center for Education Statistics Common Core of Data for the selected districts and years. The data gathered include total district population; population by race/ethnicity (black, Latino, and white); federal revenue, state revenue, and local revenue for each district; and percentage of students eligible for free lunch. For data on school districts that have been taken over, including the time period of a takeover, I rely primarily on the Education Commission of the States (2004), which has a database of state takeovers between 1989 and 2004. For state takeovers after 2004, I searched for takeovers in each state that currently has a law that allows for state takeovers.

Since the dependent variable is dichotomous, I use a logistic regression to examine the factors associated with state takeovers. Although the logit model is appropriate for this analysis, standard logit models have a limited causal inference protection, and there may be some underlying selection mechanism that may prevent us from estimating the direct effect of some of the independent variables in the model. Thus, the results of the analysis point to correlations between the variables of interest rather than causal claims.

For access to data for replication purposes, visit https://domingomorel. com/data-2/.

CHAPTER 1

1. The Boston, Chicago, and New York City schools were taken over by their respective states before school governance authority was given to their mayors. See appendix A for discussion on state takeovers and mayoral control.
2. See appendix B for a list of state takeovers of local school districts.
3. Wong and Shen (2003) provide an examination of the effects of state takeovers on educational outcomes in the early period of state takeovers (1990–2000). For an analysis on the effects of state takeovers on educational outcomes between 2010 and 2015, see the report by the Annenberg Institute for School Reform, "Investing in What Works: Community-Driven Strategies for Strong Public Schools in Georgia" (2015).
4. The Georgia state legislature approved a measure to place a referendum on a state-wide ballot to give the governor authority to take over school districts, but in 2016, Georgia voters rejected the measure.

CHAPTER 2

1. Newark school board meeting minutes, June 26, 1990.
2. Marion Bolden, interview by the author.
3. Interview by the author.
4. Interview by the author.
5. Interview by the author.
6. Newark school board meeting minutes, May 28, 1996.
7. Ibid.
8. The School Improvement Grants (SIG) program is a federal grant system that targets the lowest-performing districts in each state. The program was originally created and authorized under the Elementary and Secondary Education Act of 1965. State education agencies in every state announce the lowest-performing schools, making them eligible for the SIG, and then the local education agencies determine how they will seek the funds. In order to receive a SIG, localities have to choose a school improvement plan from four available options. After weeks of turmoil, the Central Falls teachers union, school board, and superintendent agreed on an intervention method that resulted in the "rehiring" of teachers and administrative staff.

9. Puerto Ricans, although not foreign-born, represent 10 percent of the city's population.
10. Some analysts estimate that the number of Latinos in Central Falls is considerably larger than the census figures due to the number of undocumented immigrants who reside in the city (see Holland 2010).
11. Keith Oliveira, interview by the author.
12. Interview by the author.
13. The comments were made by mayoral candidates in a 2005 forum organized by the Rhode Island Latino Civic Fund.
14. Interview by the author.
15. Anna Cano Morales, interview by the author.
16. Peter McWalters, interview by the author.
17. James Diossa, interview by the author.

CHAPTER 3

1. This claim is based on my analysis of state takeovers of local school districts using the data set I compiled.
2. The historical frame is building on the work of Pierson (2004), who argues that incorporating temporal dimensions into research analysis is essential to understanding and explaining political outcomes.
3. See appendix C for the Newark case study data sources.
4. The average population size of the cities that have been taken over is 225,550 (Newark's population 277,000). Over 80 percent of takeovers occur in districts like Newark, where blacks and Latinos represent the majority of the population.
5. Some voices in the African American community opposed the state takeover plan; they argued that blacks were poised to control the district in the near future without the help of a state takeover (Rich 1996).
6. Newark school board meeting, August 13, 1991.
7. Newark school board meeting, August 27, 1991.
8. Newark school board meeting minutes, October 1995.
9. "Essex County School Elections," *Star-Ledger*. See "School Board Candidate Profiles," *Star-Ledger*, April 11, 2002; "The Candidates for School Board," *Star-Ledger*, April 10, 2003.
10. Ibid.
11. Eighty percent of state takeover laws were passed by Republican governors.
12. For the list of state takeovers of local school districts, I relied primarily on the Education Commission of the States. I collected racial/ethnic descriptive representation data for the school board in each district that was taken over by the state dating back to 1989. For African American representation, I relied on the National Roster of Black Elected Officials by the Joint Center for Political and Economic Studies. For Latino representation, I relied on the Directory of Latino Elected Officials provided by the National Association of Latino Elected and Appointed Officials. For descriptive representation data not accessible through the National Roster of Black Elected Officials or the Directory of Latino Elected Officials, I used a combination of strategies, including online and newspaper sources, as well as

acquiring data directly from a particular city or school district. I relied on state and county boards of elections for election data. For the partisan makeup of the state governorships I relied on data from the National Governors Association. See appendix D for additional details on data sources.

CHAPTER 4

1. Adolph Reed defines a black-led regime as a "black-led and black dominated administration backed by solid council majorities" (1999, 79).
2. Paul Manna defines "license" as the "strength of the arguments available to justify government action" (2006, 14).
3. "Governors Get Serious about Schools," *New York Times*, August 28, 1986, p. A22.
4. For a summary of the literature on state takeovers in the 1990s, see the Institute on Education Law and Policy 2002.
5. The figure is arrived at by calculating every student who attends public schools (traditional public and public charter) in a city that has experienced a state takeover of the local school district compared with the entire black public student population in the state.
6. See appendix D for notes on data sources and analysis.
7. I use a logistic regression to examine the factors associated with state takeovers of local school districts. See appendix D for discussion on the limits of standard logit regression models.
8. For research on school closures, see De la Torre and Gwynne 2009; Good 2017; Lee and Lubienski 2016; MacDonald, Steinberg, and Scull 2015; Schiller 2015; Toneff-Cotner and Galletta 2016.

CHAPTER 5

1. To analyze the Newark case study, several data sources were used. I relied primarily on the U.S. Census for demographic data. I used several newspaper sources, most notably the *Star-Ledger* and the *New York Times*, for historical and contemporary data. I relied on documents from the Essex County Clerk's Office, New Jersey Department of Education, New Jersey Department of State, and Newark Public Schools for voting records, teaching and staff data, and school board meeting minutes to conduct content analysis. I also conducted 44 interviews of state officials, district administrators, teachers, parents, and local leaders. Finally, I attended Newark school board meetings during the 2012–2013 school year.
2. In 2013 Beverly Hall was indicted for participating in a cheating scandal in the Atlanta Public Schools.
3. Marion Bolden, interview by the author.
4. Ibid.
5. Ibid.
6. Interview by the author, October 14, 2013.
7. Bolden, interview by the author.
8. Richard Cammarieri, interview by the author.
9. Newark Public Schools Advisory Board minutes.

10. The 1995 state takeover of the Newark schools occurred when Sharpe James, Booker's predecessor, was already mayor.
11. Bolden, interview by the author.
12. Newark Public Schools Advisory Board meeting, September 28, 2010.
13. Newark Public Schools Advisory Board meeting, June 19, 2012.
14. Author's log from 2012–2013 advisory board meetings.
15. Newark Public Schools Advisory Board meeting minutes.
16. Ibid.
17. Antoinette Baskerville-Richardson, interview by the author.
18. Newark Public Schools Advisory Board meeting, April 23, 2013.

CHAPTER 6
1. Newark Public Schools Advisory Board meeting minutes, July 23, 1996.
2. Newark Public Schools Advisory Board meeting minutes, February 13, 1997.
3. Newark Public Schools Advisory Board meeting minutes, February 25 and March 25, 1997.
4. Marion Bolden, interview by the author.

EPILOGUE
1. Ras Baraka, interview by the author.
2. Ibid.

REFERENCES

Agranoff, R., and M. McGuire. 1998. "The Intergovernmental Context of Local Economic Development." *State and Local Government Review* 30:150–164.

Alaya, A. 1998. "Newark Mayor Plans Summit to Free City Schools from State." *Star-Ledger*, April 5.

Alaya, A. 1999. "Newark School Chief Leaves a Daunting Mission Unfinished—Hall Says She Built a Base for Success." *Star-Ledger*, June 20.

Alexander, Michelle. 2010. *The New Jim Crow: Mass Incarceration in the Age of Colorblindness*. New York: New Press.

Allen, Danielle. 2016. *Education and Equality*. Chicago, IL: University of Chicago Press.

Andrews, Donald, Andrew Washington, Ashagre Yigletu, and Saviour Nwachukwu. 2003. "Influence of Poverty on Educational Performance in Louisiana: Emphasis on the Mississippi Delta Parishes." *Southwestern Economic Review* 30:35–44.

Annenberg Institute for School Reform. 2015. "Investing in What Works: Community-Driven Strategies for Strong Public Schools in Georgia." December. Providence, RI.

Ansell, Chris, Sarah Reckhow, and Andrew Kelly. 2009. "How to Reform a Reform Coalition: Outreach, Agenda Expansion, and Brokerage in Urban School Reform." *Policy Studies Journal* 37:717–743.

Anyon, J. 1997. *Ghetto Schooling: A Political Economy of Urban Educational Reform*. New York: Teachers College Press.

Association for Children of New Jersey. 2000. "Newark Kids Count 2000: A Profile of Child Well-Being." http://acnj.org/downloads/2000_01_01_NewarkCityReport.pdf (last accessed May 29, 2016).

Association for Children of New Jersey. 2008. "Newark Kids Count 2008: A City Profile of Child Well-Being." http://acnj.org/downloads/2008_01_01_NewarkCityReport.pdf (accessed September 7, 2016).

Bachrach, Peter, and Morton Baratz. 1962. "The Two Faces of Power." *American Political Science Review* 56(4):947–952.

Banfield, Edward, and James Wilson. 1963. *City Politics*. New York: Vintage.

Barrilleaux, C., and M. Berkman. 2003. "Do Governors Matter? Budgeting Rules and the Politics of State Policymaking." *Political Research Quarterly* 56(4):409–417.

Bartley, Numan, and Hugh Graham. 1975. *Southern Politics and the Second Reconstruction*. Baltimore, MD: Johns Hopkins University Press.

Bernick, E., and C. Wiggins. 1991. "Executive-Legislative Relations: The Governor's Role as Chief Legislator." In *Gubernatorial Leadership and State Policy*, ed. E. Herzik and B. Brown, 73–92. New York: Greenwood Press.

Berry, Frances, and William Berry. 1990. "State Lottery Adoptions as Policy Innovations: An Event History Analysis." *American Political Science Review* 84(2): 395–415.

Black, Earl. 1976. *Southern Governors and Civil Rights: Racial Segregation as a Campaign Issue in the Second Reconstruction*. Cambridge, MA: Harvard University Press.

Bluestein, Greg, and Tamar Hallerman. 2016. "The Battle over Nathan Deal's School Takeover Plan Is about to Heat Up." *Atlanta Journal Constitution*, June 28. http://politics.blog.ajc.com/2016/06/28/the-battle-over-nathan-deals-school-takeover-plan-is-about-to-heat-up/ (accessed October 24, 2016).

Bobo, Lawrence, and Franklin Gilliam. 1990. "Race, Sociopolitical Participation, and Black Empowerment." *American Political Science Review* 84:377–393.

Borg, Linda. 2015. "Central Falls Board Picks Former Assistant as New Superintendent of Schools." *Providence Journal*, April 13.

Braun, R. 1991. "State Suspends Monitoring of School Districts, Weakens Takeover Threat." *Star-Ledger*, January 13.

Bridges, A. 1984. *A City in the Republic*. New York: Cambridge University Press.

Browning, Rufus, Dale Marshall, and David Tabb. 1984. *Protest Is Not Enough: The Struggle of Blacks and Hispanics for Equality in Urban Politics*. Berkeley, CA: University of California Press.

Burch, Traci. 2013. *Trading Democracy for Justice: Criminal Convictions and the Decline of Neighborhood Political Participation*. Chicago, IL: University of Chicago Press.

Burns, N., L. Evans, G. Gamm, and C. McConnaughy. 2009. "Urban Politics in the State Arena." *Studies in American Political Development* 23:1–22.

Burns, P. 2002. "The Intergovernmental Regime and Public Policy in Hartford, Connecticut." *Journal of Urban Affairs* 24(1):55–73.

Burns, P. 2003. "Regime Theory, State Government, and a Takeover of Urban Education." *Journal of Urban Affairs* 25(3):285–303.

Calefati, J. 2011. "Christie: Newark Schools to Remain in State Hands." *Star-Ledger*, May 5.

Calefati, J. 2013. "Newark Board Votes 'No-Confidence' in Schools Chief Cami Anderson." *Star-Ledger*, April 25.

Carr, Sarah. 2014. *Hope against Hope: Three Schools, One City, and the Struggle to Educate America's Children*. New York: Bloomsbury Press.

Carter, Barry. 1995. "Newarkers React to School Takeover with Mixture of Anger and Hope." *Star-Ledger*, July 13.

Carter, Dan. 1995. *The Politics of Rage: George Wallace, the Origins of the New Conservatism, and the Transformation of American Politics*. New York: Simon and Schuster.

Casey, Leo, Matthew Di Carlo, Burnie Bond, and Esther Quintero. 2015. *The State of Teacher Diversity in American Education*. Washington, DC: Albert Shanker Institute.

Chambers, Stefanie. 2006. *Mayors and Schools: Minority Voices and Democratic Tensions in Urban Education*. Philadelphia, PA: Temple University Press.

Chiles, N. 1996. "Newark School Reorganization Cuts 634 Jobs." *Star-Ledger*, July 20.

Cody, Anthony. 2014. "Newark Mayoral Candidate Ras Baraka: 'I Will Lead a Full Scale Campaign for Local Control of Schools.'" *Education Week*, May 6. http://blogs.edweek.org/teachers/living-in-dialogue/2014/05/newark_candidate_for_mayor_ras.html (accessed June 29, 2014).

Colburn, D. 2001. "Running for Office: African-American Mayors from 1967–1996." In *African-American Mayors: Race, Politics, and the American City*, ed. D. Colburn and J. Adler, 23–56. Champagne, IL: University of Illinois Press.

Conlan, T. 1998. *From New Federalism to Devolution: Twenty-Five Years of Intergovernmental Reform*. Washington, DC: Brookings Institution Press.

Cowen Institute for Public Education Initiatives. 2013. "K–12 Public Education through the Public's Eye: Voters' Perception of Public Education." Research Brief, April. http://www.coweninstitute.com/wp-content/uploads/2013/04/public-opinion-poll-04.26.13-final1.pdf (accessed March 17, 2017).

Crain, Robert L. 1966. "Fluoridation: Diffusion of an Innovation among Cities." *Social Forces* 44(4):467–476.

Cruz, José. 1998. *Identity and Power: Puerto Rican Politics and the Challenge of Ethnicity*. Philadelphia, PA: Temple University Press.

Cunningham, John. 1966. *Newark*. Newark, NJ: New Jersey Historical Society.

Curvin, Robert. 2014. *Inside Newark: Decline, Rebellion, and the Search for Transformation*. New Brunswick, NJ: Rutgers University Press.

Dahl, Robert. 1961. *Who Governs? Democracy and Power in an American City*. New Haven, CT: Yale University Press.

Dawson, Michael. 2001. *Black Visions: The Roots of Contemporary African-American Political Ideologies*. Chicago, IL: University of Chicago Press.

De la Torre, Marisa, and Julia Gwynne. 2009. "When Schools Close: Effects on Displaced Students in Chicago Public Schools." Research Report. Chicago, IL: Consortium on Chicago School Research.

DePalma, A. 1990. "Newark's New Image Buoys Mayor on Eve of Election." *New York Times*, May 4.

Dye, Thomas. 1990. *American Federalism: Competition among Governments*. Lexington, KY: Lexington Books.

Education Alliance and the Annenberg Institute for School Reform. 2013. *Third Year Transformation Report*. October. Providence, RI.

Education Commission of the States. 2004. "State Takeovers and Reconstitutions." Denver, CO.

Elkin, S. L. 1987. *City and Regime in the American Republic*. Chicago, IL: University of Chicago Press.

Elliott, W. 2013. "Newark School Board Rejects Budget." *LocalTalkNews.com*, April 8.

Epstein, Kitty K. 2012. *A Different View of Urban Schools: Civil Rights, Critical Race Theory, and Unexplored Realities*. 2nd edition. New York: Peter Lang.

Erie, Steven. 1988. *Rainbow's End: Irish-Americans and the Dilemmas of Urban Machine Politics, 1840–1985*. Berkeley, CA: University of California Press.

Espinosa, S. 1991. "Regents' Leader Says Law Lets State Take Over Central Falls Schools." *Providence Journal*, April 27.

Fraga, Luis, Kenneth Meier, and Robert England. 1986. "Hispanic Americans and Educational Policy: Limits to Equal Access." *Journal of Politics* 48:850–876.

Frug, G., and D. Barron. 2008. *City Bound: How States Stifle Urban Innovation*. Ithaca, NY: Cornell University Press.

Fung, Archon. 2004. *Empowered Participation: Reinventing Urban Democracy*. Princeton, NJ: Princeton University Press.

Gaboraug, Andrea. 2015. "The Myth of the New Orleans School Makeover." *New York Times*, August 22.

Giambusso, David. 2013. "Newark Council Votes for Moratorium on Public School Initiatives." *Star-Ledger*, May 2.

Gillespie, A. 2012. *The New Black Politician: Corey Booker, Newark, and Post-racial America*. New York: New York University Press.

Gladwell, Malcolm. 2015. "Starting Over: Many Katrina Victims Left New Orleans for Good. What Can We Learn from Them?" *New Yorker*, August 24. http://www.newyorker.com/magazine/2015/08/24/starting-over-dept-of-social-studies-malcolm-gladwell (last accessed December 12, 2016).

Golin, Steve. 2002. *The Newark Teachers Strike: Hopes on the Line*. New Brunswick, NJ: Rutgers University Press.

Good, Ryan. 2017. "Invoking Landscapes of Spatialized Inequality: Race, Class, and Place in Philadelphia's School Closure Debate." *Journal of Urban Affairs* 39(3):358–380.

Goodnough, Abby. 1996. "In Newark, a Hard Look at Special Education and Social Workers." *New York Times*, August 18.

Gray, Virginia. 1973. "Innovation in the States: A Diffusion Study." *American Political Science Review* 67(4):1174–1185.

Green, Robert, and Bradley Carl. 2000. "A Reform for Troubled Times: Takeovers of Urban Schools." *Annals of the American Academy of Political and Social Science* 59:56–70.

Greenhouse, S., and S. Dillon. 2010. "School's Shake-Up Is Embraced by the President." *New York Times*, March 6.

Greenstone, David, and Paul Peterson. 1973. *Race and Authority in Urban Politics: Community Participation and the War on Poverty*. New York: Russell Sage.

Haddon, H. 2013. "Newark's Book of James: A Former Mayor Returns from Prison with a Memoir—and Some Endorsements." *Wall Street Journal*, October 8.

Hall, Beverly. 1996. "Newark School Plan Will Make Kids the First Consideration." *Star-Ledger*, July 24.

Hanson, Russell. 1998. "The Interaction of State and Local Government." In *Governing Partners: State-Local Relations in the United States*, ed. Russell L. Hanson, 1–16. Boulder, CO: Westview Press.

Hardy-Fanta, Carol, Christine Sierra, Pei-te Lien, Dianne Pinderhughes, and Wartyna Davis. 2005. "Race, Gender, and Descriptive Representation: An Exploratory View of Multicultural Elected Leadership in the United States." Paper presented at the Annual Meeting of the American Political Science Association, Washington, DC.

Harris, Douglas, and Matthew Larsen. 2016. "The Effects of the New Orleans Post-Katrina School Reforms on Student Academic Outcomes." New Orleans, LA: Education Research Alliance for New Orleans.

Harrison, Elizabeth. 2013. "Central Falls High School, Three Years after a Mass Firing." Rhode Island Public Radio, December 31. http://ripr.org/post/central-falls-high-school-three-years-after-mass-firing.

Hartz, Louis. 1955. *The Liberal Tradition in America: An Interpretation of American Political Thought since the Revolution*. San Diego, CA: Harcourt.

Hedge, D. 1998. *Governance and the Changing American States*. Boulder, CO: Westview Press.

Henig, Jeffrey. 2013. *The End of Exceptionalism in American Education: The Changing Politics of School Reform*. Cambridge, MA: Harvard Education Press.

Henig, Jeffrey, Richard Hula, Marion Orr, and Desiree Pedescleaux. 2001. *The Color of School Reform: Race, Politics, and the Challenge of Urban Education*. Princeton, NJ: Princeton University Press.

Herbes, John. 1986. "Governors Seek Greater Authority over Operation of Public Schools: Governors Seek More Control over Public Schools." *New York Times*, August 24, p. 1.

Herman, Max. 2005. *Fighting in the Streets: Ethnic Succession and Urban Unrest in Twentieth-Century America*. New York: Peter Lang Publishing, Inc.

Herrington, Carolyn, and Frances Fowler. 2003. "Rethinking the Role of States and Educational Governance." In *American Educational Governance on Trial: Change and Challenges, Part I*, ed. William Lowe Boyd and Debra Miretsky, 271–290. Chicago, IL: University of Chicago Press.

Hochschild, Jennifer L., and Nathan Scovronick. 2004. *The American Dream and Public Schools*. New York: Oxford University Press.

Holland, William. 2010. *A School in Trouble: A Personal Story of Central Falls High School*. Lanham, MD: Rowman and Littlefield.

Holzman, Michael. 2010. "Yes We Can: The Schott 50 State Report on Public Education and Black Males." Cambridge, MA: Schott Foundation for Public Education.

Hong, Soo. 2011. *A Cord of Three Strands: A New Approach to Parent Engagement in Schools*. Cambridge, MA: Harvard Education Press.

Horan, C. 2002. "Racializing Regime Politics." *Journal of Urban Affairs* 24(1):19–33.

Hunter, Floyd. 1953. *Community Power Structure*. New York: Doubleday.

Imbroscio, D. L. 1998. "Reformulating Urban Regime Theory: The Division of Labor between State and Market Revisited." *Journal of Urban Affairs* 20:233–248.

Institute on Education Law and Policy. 2002. *Developing a Plan for Reestablishing Local Control in the State-Operated School Districts: A Final Report Submitted to the New Jersey Department of Education*. http://ielp.rutgers.edu/docs/developing_plan_full.pdf (accessed August 11, 2014).

Joseph, Peniel. 2015. *Stokley: A Life*. New York: Basic Books.

Kaestle, Carl. 1983. *Pillars of the Republic: Common Schools and American Society*. New York: Hill and Wang.

Kantor, Paul. 1988. *The Dependent City: The Changing Political Economy of Urban America*. Glenview, IL: Scott, Foresman/Little Brown.

Kantor, Paul, H. V. Savitch, and Serena V. Haddock. 1997. "The Political Economy of Urban Regimes." *Urban Affairs Review* 32:348–377.

Kapeluck, Branwell, Robert Steed, and Laurence Moreland. 2006. "Southern Governors and Legislatures." In *Writing Southern Politics: Contemporary Interpretations and*

Future Directions, ed. Robert Steed and Laurence Moreland, 269–290. Lexington, KY: University Press of Kentucky.

Karnig, Albert, and Susan Welch. 1980. *Black Representation and Urban Policy*. Chicago, IL: University of Chicago Press.

Katznelson, Ira, and Margaret Weir. 1985. *Schooling for All: Class, Race, and the Decline of the Democratic Ideal*. New York: Basic Books.

Kaufmann, Karen. 2004. *The Urban Voter: Group Conflict and Mayoral Voting Behavior in American Cities*. Ann Arbor, MI: University of Michigan Press.

Kirp, David. 2013. *Improbable Scholars: The Rebirth of a Great American School System and a Strategy for America's Schools*. New York: Oxford University Press.

Kirst, M. 1984. *Who Controls Our Schools?* New York: W. H. Freeman and Company.

Krasovic, Mark. 2016. *The Newark Frontier: Community Action in the Great Society*. Chicago, IL: University of Chicago Press.

Kraus, N. 2004. "The Significance of Race in Urban Politics: The Limitations of Regime Theory." *Race and Society* 7(2):95–111.

Kukla, B. 1996. "School Employees Mobilize for Protest." *Star-Ledger*, June 13.

Lacour, Misty, and Laura Tissington. 2011. "The Effects of Poverty on Academic Achievement." *Educational Research and Reviews* 6(7):522–527.

LaNoue, G., and B. Smith. 1973. *The Politics of School Decentralization*. Washington, DC: Heath and Company.

Larini, Rudy. 1995. "'No-Nonsense' Boss Named for District." *Star-Ledger*, July 6.

Larini, Rudy, Matthew Reilly, and Lisa Peterson. 1995. "State Takes Control of Newark Schools." *Star-Ledger*, July 13.

Lee, Jin, and Christopher Lubienski. 2016. "The Impact of School Closures on Equity of Access in Chicago." *Education and Urban Society* 49(1):53–80.

Lerman, Amy, and Vesla Weaver. 2014. *Arresting Citizenship: The Democratic Consequences of American Crime Control*. Chicago, IL: University of Chicago Press.

Lester, J., and E. Lombard. 1998. "Environmental Regulation and State-Local Relations." In *Governing Partners: State-Local Relations in the United States*, ed. R. Hanson, 139–160. Boulder, CO: Westview Press.

Lilley, Robert, Raymond Brown, John Dougherty, Alfred Driscoll, John Gibbons, Ben Leuchter, Oliver Lofton, Robert Meyner, Prince Taylor, and William Wachenfeld. 1968. *Governor's Select Commission on Civil Disorder*. Report for Action. New York: Lemma Publishing.

Lowndes, Joseph. 2008. *From the New Deal to the New Right: Race and the Southern Origins of Modern Conservatism*. New Haven, CT: Yale University Press.

Lucas, Caryl. 1995. "Ousted Chief Quietly Exits the Stage." *Star-Ledger*, July 13.

Lucas, Caryl. 1996. "Fired (Up) Newark School Employees See Racism, Cronyism, Politics at Work." *Star-Ledger*, July 20.

MacDonald, John, Matthew Steinberg, and Janie Scull. 2015. "The Direct and Indirect Effects of Closing Schools on Students' Educational Settings: Evidence from Two Rounds of School Closures in Philadelphia." Paper presented at the Annual Meeting of the Association for Public Policy Analysis and Management, Miami, FL, November 14.

Malinowski, W. Zachary. 2014. "Central Falls Mayor James Diossa Sworn in for First Multi-year Term." *Providence Journal*, January 7.

Manna, Paul. 2006. *School's In: Federalism and National Education Agenda*. Washington, DC: Georgetown University Press.

Manna, P. 2011. *Collision Course: Federal Education Policy Meets State and Local Realities*. Washington, DC: CQ Press.

Marschall, Melissa. 2005. "Minority Incorporation and Local School Boards." In *Besieged: School Boards and the Future of Education Politics*, ed. W. Howell, 173–198. Washington, DC: Brookings Institution Press.

Marschall, Melissa, and Anirudh Ruhil. 2007. "Substantive Symbols: The Attitudinal Dimension of Black Political Incorporation." *American Journal of Political Science* 51:17–33.

Mayer, Jane. 2016. *Dark Money: The Hidden History of the Billionaires Behind the Rise of the Radical Right*. New York, NY: Anchor Books.

McCoy, C. 1988. "State Moves Closer to Newark School Takeover." *Philadelphia Inquirer*, January 15.

McDermott, K. 1999. *Controlling Public Education: Localism versus Equity*. Lawrence, KS: University Press of Kansas.

McDermott, K. 2011. *High-Stakes Reform: The Politics of Educational Accountability*. Washington, DC: Georgetown University Press.

McLarin, K. 1994. "New Jersey Prepares a Takeover of Newark's Desperate Schools." *New York Times*, July 23.

McMillen, Neil. 1971. *The Citizens' Council: Organized Resistance to the Second Reconstruction, 1954–1964*. Urbana, IL: University of Illinois Press.

Meier, Kenneth. 2013. "From Theory to Results in Governance Reform." In *Education Governance for the Twenty-First Century: Overcoming the Structural Barriers to School Reform*, ed. P. Manna and P. McGuinn, 353–374. Washington, DC: Brookings Institution.

Meier, Kenneth, and Robert England. 1984. "Black Representation and Educational Policy: Are They Related?" *American Political Science Review* 78:392–403.

Meier, Kenneth, and Laurence J. O'Toole. 2006. *Bureaucracy in a Democratic State: A Governance Perspective*. Baltimore, MD: Johns Hopkins University Press.

Mettler, Suzanne. 1998. *Dividing Citizens: Gender and Federalism in New Deal Public Policy*. Ithaca, NY: Cornell University Press.

Mills, C. Wright. 1959. *The Power Elite*. Reprint. New York: Oxford University Press, 1975.

Mintrom, Michael. 1997. "Policy Entrepreneurs and the Diffusion of Innovation." *American Journal of Political Science* 41(3):738–770.

Mintrom, Michael, and Sandra Vergari. 1998. "Policy Networks and Innovation Diffusion: The Case of State Education Reforms." *Journal of Politics* 60(1):126–148.

Mirel, Jeffrey. 2004. "Detroit: "There Is Still a Long Road to Travel, and Success Is Far from Assured." In *Mayors in the Middle: Politics, Race, and Mayoral Control of Urban Schools*, ed. Jeffrey Henig and Wilbur Rich, 120–158. Princeton, NJ: Princeton University Press.

Mondics, C. 1993. "Whitman Appoints Chief of Education She Says She Will Rely on Leo Klagholz to Carry Out Her Plans to Raise Standards and Tighten Financial Controls." *Philadelphia Inquirer*, December 14.

Mooney, J. 2013. "How Have Newark's Schools Fared under Cory Booker?" *NJ Spotlight*, October 11.

Moore, Leonard. 2003. *Carl B. Stokes and the Rise of Black Political Power*. Champaign, IL: University of Illinois Press.

Morel, Domingo, and Jennifer Cassidy. 2011. "Do Weak Local Institutions Invite Federal Attention? Prospects for Education Reform." Paper presented at the Annual Meeting of the American Political Science Association, Seattle, WA.

Morone, James. 1990. *The Democratic Wish: Popular Participation and the Limits of American Government*. New Haven, CT: Yale University Press.

Moynihan, Daniel. 1969. *Maximum Feasible Misunderstanding: Community Action in the War on Poverty*. New York: Free Press.

Mumford, Kevin. 2007. *Newark: A History of Race, Rights, and Riots in America*. New York: New York University Press.

Murphy, Jerome. 1973. *State Education Agencies and Discretionary Funds: Grease the Squeaky Wheel*. Lanham, MD: Lexington Books.

National Advisory Commission on Civil Disorders. 1968. *Report of the National Advisory Commission on Civil Disorders*. New York: Bantam Books.

National Commission on Excellence in Education. 1983. *A Nation at Risk: The Imperative for Educational Reform: A Report to the Nation and the Secretary of Education, United States Department of Education*. Washington, DC.

Nelson, W. 2000. *Black Atlantic Politics: Dilemmas of Political Empowerment in Boston and Liverpool*. Albany, NY: SUNY Press.

Nelson, W., and P. Meranto. 1977. *Electing Black Mayors: Political Action in the Black Community*. Columbus, OH: Ohio State University Press.

Newman, M. 1999. "New Jersey Finds No Simple Solutions in School Takeovers." *New York Times*, March 21.

Nice, D. 1998. "The Intergovernmental Setting of State-Local Relations." In *Governing Partners: State-Local Relations in the United States*, ed. R. Hanson, 17–36. Boulder, CO: Westview Press.

Nix, Naomi. 2015. "20 Years of Debate: State Control of Newark Schools Entering Third Decade." NJ.com, April 13. http://www.nj.com/essex/index.ssf/2015/04/newark_schools_takeover.html.

Noguera, Pedro. 2003. *City Schools and the American Dream: Reclaiming the Promise of Public Education*. New York: Teachers College Press.

Nuamah, Sally. 2018, forthcoming. "The Paradox of Educational Attitudes: Racial Differences in Public Opinion on School Closures." *Journal of Urban Affairs*.

Ogletree, Charles. 2014. "The Legacy and Implications of San Antonio Independent School District v. Rodriguez." *Richmond Journal of Law and the Public Interest* 17(2):515–548.

Oluwole, J., and P. Green. 2009. "State Takeovers of School Districts: Race and the Equal Protection Clause." *Indiana Law Review* 42(2):343–409.

Orfield, Gary, and Susan Eaton. 1996. *Dismantling Desegregation: The Quiet Reversal of "Brown v. Board of Education."* New York: New Press.

Orr, Marion. 1992. "Urban Regimes and Human Capital Policies: A Study of Baltimore." *Journal of Urban Affairs* 14:173–187.

Orr, Marion. 1999. *Black Social Capital: The Politics of School Reform in Baltimore, 1986–1998*. Lawrence: University Press of Kansas.

Owens, Ann, Sean Reardon, and Christopher Jencks. 2016. "Income Segregation between Schools and School Districts." *American Education Research Journal* 53(4):1159–1197.

Owens, Michael, and Jacob Brown. 2013. "Weakening Strong Black Political Empowerment: Implications from Atlanta's 2009 Mayoral Election." *Journal of Urban Affairs* 36:663–681.

Pantoja, Adrian, and Gary Segura. 2003. "Does Ethnicity Matter? Descriptive Representation in Legislatures and Political Alienation among Latinos." *Social Science Quarterly* 84:441–459.

Peterson, L. 1995. "State Comes in and Officials Go out in Scene with Little Confrontation." *Star-Ledger*, July 13.

Pew Hispanic Center. 2002. " Latino Growth in Metropolitan America: Changing Patterns, New Locations." Washington, DC: Brookings Institution. http://pewhispanic.org/files/reports/10.pdf.

Pierson, Paul. 2004. *Politics in Time: History, Institutions, and Social Analysis*. Princeton, NJ: Princeton University Press.

Pierson, Paul, and Theda Skocpol. 2007. "American Politics in the Long Run." In *The Transformation of American Politics: Activist Government and the Rise of Conservatism*, ed. Paul Pierson and Theda Skocpol, 3–16. Princeton, NJ: Princeton University Press.

Pinderhughes, Dianne. 1987. *Race and Ethnicity in Chicago Politics*. Chicago, IL: University of Illinois Press.

Pizarro, Max. 2015. "Christie and Baraka Unveil 'Newark Educational Success Board.'" *Observer*, June 26. http://observer.com/2015/06/christie-and-baraka-unveil-newark-educational-success-board/ (last accessed April 22, 2017).

Pratt, R. 1992. "New Jersey State Department of Education Monitoring, Intervention, and Takeover Practices in the Newark, Trenton, and Jersey City Public School Districts." Ed.D. thesis, Seton Hall University.

Quinn, L. 1988. "Camden District Praised for Efforts." *Philadelphia Inquirer*, May 25.

Rabig, Julia. 2016. *The Fixers: Devolution, Development, and Civil Society in Newark, 1960-1990*. Chicago, IL: University of Chicago Press.

Rangel, Jesus. 1988. "Extortion of Teachers Is Charged." *New York Times*, November 1.

Ravitch, Diane. 2000. *The Great School Wars: A History of the New York City Public Schools*. Baltimore, MD: Johns Hopkins University Press.

Reagan, Michael. 1972. *The New Federalism*. New York: Oxford University Press.

Reardon, Sean. 2011. "The Widening Academic Gap between the Rich and the Poor: New Evidence and Possible Explanations." In *Whither Opportunity? Rising Inequality, Schools, and Children's Life Chances*, ed. Richard Murnane and Greg Duncan, 91–116. New York: Russell Sage Foundation.

Reckhow, Sarah. 2013. *Follow the Money: How Foundation Dollars Change Public School Politics*. New York: Oxford University Press.

Reed, Adolph. 1999. *Stirrings in the Jug: Black Politics in the Post-Segregation Era*. Minneapolis, MN: University of Minnesota Press.

Reed, Douglas. 2001. *On Equal Terms: The Constitutional Politics of Educational Opportunity*. Princeton, NJ: Princeton University Press.

Reid, Karla. 2001. "'Comeback' from State Control Means Solvency for Compton." *Education Week* 20(20):1.

Reilly, Matthew. 1995. "Judge Halts Takeover of Newark Schools." *Star-Ledger*, July 6.

Rich, Wilbur. 1996. *Black Mayors and School Politics: The Failure of Reform in Detroit, Gary, and Newark*. New York: Garland Publishing, Inc.

Rich, Wilbur. 1999. *Coleman Young and Detroit Politics: From Social Activist to Power Broker*. Detroit, MI: Wayne State University Press.

Rich, Wilbur. 2006. *David Dinkins and New York City Politics: Race, Images, and the Media*. Albany, NY: SUNY Press.

Rivlin, Alice. 1992. *Reviving the American Dream: The Economy, the States, and the Federal Government*. Washington, DC: Brookings Institution.

Roberts, R., T. Burroughs, K. Dilworth, and C. Lucas. 1992. "Record $523 Million School Budget for Newark Passed at Essex Polls." *Star-Ledger*, April 8.

Rocha, Rene, and Tetsuya Matsubayashi. 2013. "Latino Representation and Immigration in Local Politics." *Urban Affairs Review* 49:353–380.

Rundquist, J. 2013. "Christie to Newark: We Run the School District." *Star-Ledger*, September 5.

Russakoff, Dale. 2015. *The Prize: Who's in Charge of America's Schools?* New York: Houghton Mifflin Harcourt.

Salmore, B., and S. Salmore. 2013. *New Jersey Politics and Government: The Suburbs Come of Age*. 4th edition. New Brunswick, NJ: Rutgers University Press.

Saltzstein, Grace. 1989. "Black Mayors and Police Policies." *Journal of Politics* 51:525–544.

Schiller, Jessica. 2015. "School's Out: A Critical Look at the Impact of School Closings in Baltimore." Paper presented at the School Closures Conference at the University of Pennsylvania, Philadelphia, PA.

Schueler, Beth. 2016. "A Third Way? The Politics of School District Takeover and Turnaround in Lawrence, Massachusetts." Paper presented at the Annual Meeting of the Association of Public Policy and Analysis, Washington, DC.

Shah, Paru. 2006. "The Politics and Policy Implications of Latino Representation in Education." Ph.D. diss., Rice University.

Shah, Paru. 2009. "Motivating Participation: The Symbolic Effects of Latino Representation on Parent School Involvement." *Social Science Quarterly* 90:212–230.

Shipan, Charles, and Craig Volden. 2008. "The Mechanisms of Policy Diffusion." *American Journal of Political Science* 52(4):840–857.

Shipps, Dorothy. 2003. "Pulling Together: Civic Capacity and Urban School Reform." *American Educational Research Journal* 40:841–878.

Smothers, R. 2003. "What Is Newark Telling Sharpe James?" *New York Times*, April 20.

Spence, Lester. 2015. *Knocking the Hustle: Against the Neoliberal Turn in Black Politics*. Brooklyn, NY: Punctum Books.

State of New Jersey Department of Education. 1994. "Comprehensive Compliance Investigation Report for the Newark School District."

State of New Jersey Department of Education. 2008. "High School Proficiency Assessment." http://www.nj.gov/education/assessment/hs/hspa/results/ (accessed September 18, 2016).

State of New Jersey Department of State, Division of Elections. 2013. "2013 Election Information." http://nj.gov/state/elections/election-information-archive-2013.html#3 (accessed March 24, 2014).

Steffes, Tracy. 2012. *School, Society, and State: A New Education to Govern Modern America*. Chicago, IL: University of Chicago Press.

Stewart, Joseph, Robert England, and Kenneth Meier. 1989. "Black Representation in Urban School Districts: From School Board to Office to Classroom." *Western Political Quarterly* 42:287–305.

Stone, Clarence. 1989. *Regime Politics: Governing Atlanta, 1946–1988*. Lawrence, KS: University Press of Kansas.

Stone, Clarence. 2001. "Civic Capacity and Urban Education." *Urban Affairs Review* 36:595–619.

Stonecash, J. 2002. *The Emergence of State Government: Parties and New Jersey Politics, 1950–2000*. Madison, NJ: Fairleigh Dickinson University Press.

Sugrue, Thomas. 1996. *The Origins of the Urban Crisis: Race and Inequality in Postwar Detroit*. Princeton, NJ: Princeton University Press.

Sugrue, Thomas. 2008. *Sweet Land of Liberty: The Forgotten Struggle for Civil Rights in the North*. New York: Random House.

Tate, Katherine. 2001. "The Political Representation of Blacks in Congress: Does Race Matter?" *Legislative Studies Quarterly* 26:623–638.

Tate, Katherine. 2003. *Black Faces in the Mirror: African Americans and Their Representatives in the U.S. Congress*. Princeton, NJ: Princeton University Press.

Teaford, Jon. 2002. *The Rise of the States: Evolution of American State Government*. Baltimore, MD: Johns Hopkins University Press.

Timar, Thomas. 1997. "The Institutional Role of State Education Departments: A Historical Perspective." *American Journal of Education* 105(3):231–260.

Tocqueville, A. de. [1835] 2007. *Democracy in America*. Ed. H. Reeve. Stilwell, KS: Digireads.com.

Toneff-Cotner, Glenda, and Anne Galletta. 2016. "School Closure, Relational Trust, and Civic Bonds and Ruptures: A Current and Retrospective Study of High School Closure." Paper presented at the Annual Meeting of the Society for Research on Adolescence, Baltimore, MD, April.

Tractenberg, Paul. 1974. "*Robinson v. Cahill*: The 'Thorough and Efficient' Clause." *Law and Contemporary Problems* 38:312–332.

Tractenberg, Paul, Brenda Liss, and Alan Sadovnik. 2005. "Setting the Stage for Informed, Objective Deliberation on Property Tax Reform: What We Know, and What We Need to Know, about Education Funding and Taxes." Report from the Rutgers-Newark Institute on Education Law and Policy. Newark, NJ.

Trounstine, Jessica. 2006. "Dominant Regimes and the Demise of Urban Democracy." *Journal of Politics* 68:879–893.

Turcol, T., and A. John-Hall. 1994. "State Set to Seize Newark Schools Officials Say the System Is Mismanaged and Failing Its Students. The City Has to Show It Can Turn Things Around." *Philadelphia Inquirer*, July 23.

Tuttle, Brad. 2009. *How Newark Became Newark: The Rise, Fall, and Rebirth of an American City*. New Brunswick, NJ: Rutgers University Press.

Tyack, David. 1974. *The One Best System: A History of American Urban Education*. Cambridge, MA: Harvard University Press.

U.S. Bureau of Labor Statistics. 2010. *Local Area Unemployment Statistics*. Newark, NJ.

U.S. Census. 1990. *Census of Population and Housing*. Washington, DC: Government Printing Office.

U.S. Census. 2000. *Census of Population and Housing*. Washington, DC: Government Printing Office.

U.S. Census. 2010. *Census of Population and Housing*. Washington, DC: Government Printing Office.

U.S. Department of Education. 2001. *The Longitudinal Evaluation of School Change and Performance in Title I Schools*. Washington, DC: Government Printing Office.

Verdon, J. 1988. "When a School System Loses Control: A Primer on Political Patronage in New Jersey, No District Is More Thorough than Jersey City." *The Record*, January 10.

Vinovskis, Maris. 2008. *From a Nation at Risk to No Child Left Behind: National Education Goals and the Creation of Federal Education Policy*. New York: Teachers College Press.

Walker, Jack L. 1969. "The Diffusion of Innovations among the American States." *American Political Science Review* 63(3):880–899.

Walker, Steven. 1995. "15 Newarkers Named to Panel Advising State's School Administrators." *Star-Ledger*, September 9.

Warren, Mark, and Karen Mapp. 2011. *A Match on Dry Grass: Community Organizing as a Catalyst for School Reform*. New York: Oxford University Press.

Weaver, Vesla. 2007. "Frontlash: Race and the Development of Punitive Crime Policy." *Studies in American Political Development* 21:230–265.

Weier, Margaret. 2005. "States, Race, and the Decline of New Deal Liberalism." *Studies in American Political Development* 19:157–172.

Welch, Susan, and Albert Karnig. 1978. "Representation of Blacks on Big City School Boards." *Social Science Quarterly* 59:162–172.

Western, Bruce. 2006. *Punishment and Inequality in American Democracy*. New York: Russell Sage Foundation.

Wirt, Frederick, and Michael Kirst. 1997. *The Political Dynamics of American Education*. Berkeley, CA: McCutchan.

Wong, Kenneth, and Warren E. Langevin. 2005. "The Diffusion of Governance Reform in American Public Education: An Event History Analysis of State Takeover and Charter School Laws." National Research and Development Center on School Choice (NJ1). Nashville, TN.

Wong, Kenneth, and Francis Shen. 2003. "Measuring the Effectiveness of City and State Takeover as a School Reform Strategy." *Peabody Journal of Education* 78:89–119.

Woodward, Komozi. 1999. *A Nation within a Nation: Amiri Baraka (LeRoi Jones) and Black Power Politics*. Chapel Hill, NC: University of North Carolina Press.

Yaffe, D. 2007. *Other People's Children: The Battle for Justice and Equality in New Jersey's Schools*. New Brunswick, NJ: Rutgers University Press.

Ziebarth, Todd. 2002. "State Takeovers and Reconstitutions." Policy Brief. Denver, CO: Education Commission of the States.

DATE DUE

230804